CRITICAL STUDIES IN KURAL

SALMON BOOKS

CRITICAL STUDIES IN KURAL

Purnalingam Pillai, M. S.

SALMON BOOKS

Chennai New Delhi

SALMON BOOKS

ISBN 9789349032385

Salmon Books
No. 44, Nallathambi Street,
Triplicane, Chennai 600 005

Printed and bound in India

MJP 091

Publisher : C. Janarthanan

Publisher's Note

The legacy of a country is in its varied cultural heritage, historical literature, developments in the field of economy and science. The top nations in the world are competing in the field of science, economy and literature. This vast legacy has to be conserved and documented so that it can be bestowed to the future generation. The knowledge of this legacy is slowly getting perished in the present generation due to lack of documentation.

Keeping this in mind, the concern with retrospective acquiring of rare books has been accented recently by the burgeoning reprint industry. Salmon Books is gratified to retrieve the rare collections with a view to bring back those books that were landmarks in their time.

In this effort, a series of rare books would be republished under the banner, "Salmon Books". he books in the reprint series have been carefully selected for their contemporary usefulness as well as their historical importance within the intellectual. We reconstruct the book with slight enhancements made for better presentation, without af-fecting the contents of the original edition.

Most of the works selected for republishing covers a huge range of subjects, from history to anthropology. We believe this reprint edition will be a service to the numerous researchers and practitioners active in this fascinating field. We allow readers to experience the wonder of peering into a scholarly work of the highest order and seminal significance.

SALMON BOOKS

Born May 1866.

CONTENTS.

FOREWORD.

A few European scholars have quarried for about a century in the *El Dorado* of the Kural. Monsieur Ariel enriched the French literature with this treasury of wisdom. What he did for the French literature the Rev. Beschi did for the Italian (rather Latin) and Dr. Graul for the German. Then a galaxy of British clerics made forays in this Tamilian Golconda and appropriated as much of it as they could to ennoble their own. Among them Ellis, Drew, and Robinson were three great luminaries. The Rev. G. U. Pope availed himself of the labours of his predecessors and brought out in 1886 the classic as a whole with a metrical translation and with a useful introduction, lexicon and concordance. The Rev. John Lazarus had anticipated Dr. Pope and supplied his English rendering in prose of this *magnum opus* to the edition published a twelvemonth early by the then leading Tamil printer and publisher, W. Pushparatha Chettiar, Madras. Quite recently Mr. V. Subramania Iyer has given out his English translation thereof in prose. There is no doubt that each edition is good in its own way. But all the editors, European and Indian, have closely followed Parimelalgar's commentary with all its defects. Manakudavar's commentary, published three years ago, seems to be, in some respects, better than Parimelalgar's, and his logical arrangement of the couplets in each chapter and his sensible notes are two of its bright features. It is a pity that the other eight commentaries have not seen the light of day. The edition of Kural by the Tamil Books Publishing Society at

Kanchipuram contains prose paraphrases of many couplets interpreted in the spirit of a true Tamilian.

The aim of the present book is akin to that of the English translators of the poem, *viz.*, the popularisation of the gemmy classic among nations and races whose vernacular is not Tamil, whether in India or abroad, but I have adopted the new line of presenting its full substance in the small compass of Twelve critical studies.

It is a good sign of the times that certain Tamil publishers have printed the text in a handy form and in a handsome manner and are selling it at cheap prices. It is a boon to the Tamil people who cannot go in for costly publications, and it is hoped that every Tamilian will take this opportunity to get a copy for himself and read, mark, learn and inwardly digest and assimilate it.

M. S. P.

Srimathi Rani Lakshmi Ammani Ammal,

The Zamindarini of Marungapuri Estate, Trichinopoly District.

DEDICATED TO

SRIMATHI RANI

LAKSHMI AMMANI AMMAL AVERGAL,

THE ZAMINDARINI OF MARUNGAPURI,

TRICHINOPOLY DISTRICT,

AUTHORESS OF THE 'TIRUK-KURAL DIPA ALANKARAM'
AND PATRONESS OF ARTS AND LETTERS,
IN APPRECIATION OF THE RANI'S PROFOUND
SCHOLARSHIP IN TAMIL LANGUAGE
AND LITERATURE.

MEMOIR.

Srimathi Rani Lakshmi Ammani Ammal Avergal, the Zamindarini of Marungapuri Estate, Trichinopoly District, is a highly cultured, refined and pious lady of thirty-four years of age and a great patron of arts and letters. Like her Zamindar-Consort Sri Krishna Vijaya Poochaya Nayakar, a good scholar in English, Tamil and other kindred tongues, a great lover of music, and a famous sportsman, who bore beneficent sway for about twenty-one years and passed away in 1926 to the great regret and sorrow of his numerous subjects, friends and admirers, Rani Lakshmi is devoting her widowed leisure to the cultivation of Tamil learning and to the diffusion of Tamil literature, culture and civilisation, by encouraging hopeful scholars in indigent circumstances with pecuniary help for prosecuting their higher studies and by writing books like the 'Tirukkural Dipa Alankaram," an elaborate and lucid exposition of the world-famous and sententious Tamil classic in simple and chaste prose. Her sister, Srimathi Subhadrammani Ammal, the first wife and sweetheart of the late talented Zamindar, was an accomplished and amiable lady of great philanthropy and benefaction, and she quit the world in 1908 in her twentieth year after a quinquennium of wedded life, bemoaned by all who had known her. Her successor in the conjugal line was the fair and noble-hearted Srimathi Alagu Vellaiyammani Ammal, who too followed her in a short time after begetting a daughter. The third in that succession is the subject of this sketch, Rani Srimathi Lakshmi Ammani, our Lady Bountiful. Brought up in her teens in the different Departments of Tamil Grammar and Literature, she is now a Tamil Scholar of no mean repute and is well-posted in Vedantic lore. Her earnest heart for the uplift and amelioration of her sisters of all sorts and conditions induced her to take up the Presidentship of the Bharathi Sisters' Sangam, Trichi, and, imbued like her late lamented lord with the modern spirit, she is taking immense interest in all public movements and is a useful and energetic member of the Women's League in Madras. The only Hopeful left to inherit the Estate is Srimathi Andal Ammani, now a girl of fourteen summers, and the Estate is once again under the management of the Court of Wards. The blooming inheritrix is making rapid progress in her study of English and Tamil under able tutorships and bids fair to be the worthy daughter of her wise parents and heroic ancestors.

As the rich Zamindari of Ramnad in the Pandi land has been the house and home of many a needy but high-souled bard and minstrel, so has been and is the Zamindari of Marungapuri in the Chola country, which dates its origin in 195 A.D. and keeps its door of hospitality open to poets, poetasters, and other illustrious wits. Both Zamindaris have appraised and appreciated men of true genius and sterling worth and have rewarded them liberally. A single instance might be cited to illustrate the bountifulness of Marungapuri. One of the Poochaya Nayakars was so enamoured of the well-turned 'Pillai Tamil' sung in his honour that he bestowed on the bard Chitrambalavanar two whole villages as a gift.

The Zamindari of Marungapuri comprises at present 101 villages with a total area of 174 square miles and fetches an yearly income of a lakh of rupees. It includes many minor and nine major devastanams maintained out of the income from villages granted by the renowned Poochaya Nayakars of the royal Camblatha clan of this ancient Zamin or Palayapat. The nearest approach to this Zamindari by train is Manapparai Station, S.I.R., situated but fourteen miles to the north of the capital.

May the surviving Rani be blessed with health and long life to carry on her acts of public utility and benevolence, and may her promising daughter who is to inherit the Estate in a few years enjoy longevity and hold the helm of the State in prosperity for years and bear fruitful and illustrious progeny to rule the Estate in endless succession is the prayer of every well-wisher of the ancient Zamin of Marungapuri!

CRITICAL STUDIES IN KURAL.

OPENING STUDY I.

The name "Thiruvalluvar" means "the great man of the Valluva community" and the title "Kural" signifies the metre of the poem. Both the author and his work have borne no proper or distinctive names. Nor is anything reliable known either of his parentage, or of his career. But the work exists or is extant as a whole, unadulterated by schismatics and unimpaired or untampered with by copyists in the procession of ages. That the poet was a keen observer of nature, animate and inanimate, a diligent student of ancient classics on ahapporul and purapporul, on rhetoric and dialectic, on morality and statecraft, on agriculture and medicine, on folk-lore, tree-and-plant-lore, and on sex-psychology and erotic diplomacy, and was a practical thinker and reformer, is beyond all cavil or question. Nobody doubts his poetic artistry (*vide* Tiru-Valluva-māllai, stanza 45, 'elutthu-asai etc.') and his noble sentiments in his masterpiece of Tamil literature composed of apophthegms in brief couplets. How a close study of this anthology would benefit a modern reader deserves consideration. Does it throw any light on the pressing problems of the day? Let the reader go over the couplets 21, 322, 373, 401, 410, 440, *533*, *543*, *560*, *581*, *636*, 683, *725*, *727*, *743*, 783, *941*, to know the extent of his erudition.

> "The settled *rule of every code* requires,
> Their greatness who, renouncing all, true to their rule have stood." 21.

"Let those that need, partake your meal; guard everything that lives;
This is the chief and sum of *lore that hoarded wisdom gives*." 322.

"To self-oblivious men no praise; this rule, as highest good,
Decisive wisdom sums of *every school*." 533.

"These two—the *code renowned*, and spies,
In these let king confide as eyes." 581.

"When native subtilty combines *sound scholastic lore*
'T is subtilty surpassing all which nothing stands before." 636.

"By rule, to dialectic art your mind apply,
That in the council fearless you make an apt reply." 725.

"To those who lack the hero's eye what can the sword avail?
Or *Science* what, to those before the council keen who quail." 726.

"As shining sword before the foe which sexless being bears,
Is *science* learned by him the council's face who fears." 727.

"Height, breadth, strength, difficult access;
Science declares *a fort* must these possess." 743.

"The *learned books* court three, with wind as first; of these
As any one prevails or fails, 't will cause disease." 941.

Vide 1078 for the sugar-cane; 104, 144, 1282 for the millet; 433, 1282 for the palmyra; 216 for the fruit-bearing tree; 1008 for the poison tree; 870 for the thorn tree; 217 for the medicine tree; 274 for the rush or thicket; 1304 for the valli or the creeper; 965 for the abrus seed (Kuntri); 621 for the pakadu or cattle; 486 for the ram; 273, 599 for the tiger; 969 for the yak or wild ox or fawn; 814 for the horse; 195 for the crocodile; 678, 758, 772 for the elephant; 481, 527, for the crow and the owl; 1120 for the annam or swan, and the sensitive plant (nerunji); 490 for the kokku or heron; 1081 for the peacock and its feathers (peeli); 500 for the jackal, and 763 for the rat and the snake.

The modern reader will find in this classical poem much food for thought, reflection and action. The *theosophist* will discover the poet's theosophy in Study I. In it God is personal and impersonal and Truth. The *moralist* will be satisfied with his precepts and maxims on hate and the evil-doer. Shakespeare has,

> " Love thyself last ; cherish those hearts that hate thee,
> Corruption wins not more than honesty.
> Still in thy right hand carry gentle peace
> To silence envious tongues ; be just and fear not;
> Let all the ends thou aim'st be thy Country's,
> Thy God's and Truth's."

Vide Study VI on " Virtues and Vices."

> " *To punish wrong, with kindly benefits the doers ply,*
> Thus shame their souls ; but pass the ill unheeded by." 314.

> " With overweening pride when men with injuries assail,
> *By thine own righteous dealing* shalt thou mightily prevail." 158.

> " What fruit doth your perfection yield you say !
> *Unless to men who work you ill you good repay.*" 987.

The *social reformer* will murmur that the poet has not done justice to womankind as he praises a wife for her implicit obedience to her lord as a God and gives her no equality and liberty that the new or the smart woman fights for in these days. But he will be immensely pleased with the poet's strictures on the caste system, on toddy-drinking, gambling, and concupiscence or debauchery, on killing and flesh-eating, and with his appreciation of hospitality or feeding strangers. *Vide* the chapters bearing these titles. It was too early for a poet who had lived eighteen hundred years ago to dream of baby marriages and baby widows or to legislate for them, as the post-puberty (arivai) marriage was the only system in vogue then and that, as a result of courtship and self-choice. The poet does not recognise the necessity for any religious ceremony or sanction to bind the parties in love, as the country was not priest-ridden at that time.

The *labourite* will be delighed with the dignity of labour maintained by the author and with the sweetness of self-earned pottage. *Vide* Chapters 60-62.

> " Nothing is sweeter than to taste the *toil-won cheer*,
> Though *mess of pottage* as tasteless as the water clear." 1065.

> " Even *thin gruel is ambrosia* to him
> Who has earned it by labour." (*ibid*).

He will find satisfaction in the condemnation of poverty due to sloth and mendicancy adopted for ease and freedom.

The *religious reformer* will derive pleasure from the poet's tirade against mere formalism or ritualism and self-mortifying and sham asceticism and from the espousing of *tapas* or penitential meditation.

The *political reformer* will learn much from the chapters on state-craft, on embassy and spying, aud on the management of foes and famines.

> " Not lance gives kings the victory,
> But sceptre *swayed with equity*." 546.

The *educational reformer* will see that technical education imparted, if it is to do good, must be based on one's special aptitude and should not be determined by heredity or custom.

> " As each man's *special aptitude* is known
> Bid each man make that special work his own." 518.

Besides the knowledge, and wisdom derived by the poet from his nature studies and from his perusal or mastery of books which he has used in an ample measure in the composition of this unique work, there are direct references to his life-experiences which reflect the nobility and the mental calibre of our *vates sacer*. Three of the couplets bearing on such experiences are quoted below :

> " Of all that men acquire *we* know not any greater gain,
> Than that which by the ***birth of learned children*** *men* *obtain.*" 61,
>
> " Of all good things *we* 've scann'd with studious care
> There's naught that can with ***truthfulness*** compare." 300.
>
> " The *base* resemble men in outward form, *I* ween ;
> But counterpart exact them *I* 've never seen." 1071,

The first shows his love of children, the second exhibits his passion for veracity, and the third manifests his contempt for baseness.

In fine, the " perfect man " of Thiruvalluvar, though he resembles other mortals in the fact of his being mother-born and in the possession of parts, arms and limbs, making up the human frame, differs from them in his meritorious work and in his moral excellence.

> " All beings that live are one in circumstance of birth ;
> *Diversities of works give each his special work.*" 972.
>
> " Men are not one, because their members seem alike to outward view ;
> Similitude of kindred quality makes likeness true." 993.

Here is a clear statement contradicting the claim of superior birth set up by priesthood which has hypnotised the unthinking masses to be willing slaves and put down their desire for uplift as blasphemy and sacrilege. Able reformers like Kapilar and Ramanujar have failed to shatter the citadel of birth supremacy, but the only effective means for its demolition is the spread or dissemination of the right kind of education among the illiterate which, by inculcating liberty, equality, and fraternity, opens their mental eye to the dense darkness of ignorance into which they have been thrust from time immemorial. Here is also a caution against the foolish boast of the low and the mean and of the oppressed, suppressed and depressed classes that they resemble the other mortals in their physique and in their blood and that they have, therefore, every right to claim equality with savants, saints and sages. What divide man from man are his learning, his wealth, and his moral worth, but these are not inseparable barriers. Despite such an able advocacy of man as man, the poet alludes to *pirap-pu olukkam*, conduct arising from or due to his birth as seer's or scholar's son in the subjoined distich.

> " Though he forget, the scholar may regain his learned lore ;
> Failing in decorum due, *regard is gone for ever more.*" 134.

The *orthodox* man may, however, gloat over this apparent slip or rather innuendo and still claim the poet as perfectly his own in respect of his belief in the soul's immortality and transmigration, in the existence of worlds above and below, in the superior virtues of asceticism, and in the birth-termination by absolute renunciation.

This triple treatise of *Morality*, *Material Prosperity* and *Affection* in 133 chapters, each of ten couplets, won immediate applause in the author's lifetime. Kalladar has praised it as a moral code for the whole of humanity, irrespective of colour, creed and community, and has set forth the way of good from the world's point of view, unbiassed by any narrow sectarian prejudices. Hence its popularity all the world over—in England, Italy, France, Germany, not to speak of India. " Though dead, he yet speaketh ". " To think is to live ; and he, by whom the reality and responsibility of life on earth was thought out in all its manifold bearings and aspects, still lives in the loving memory of millions. Nineteen centuries have not diminished the weight of his authority or the vitality of his utterances. He lives, and his fame will increase with the flight of time ; and as long as men continue to revere the true and the good, will the words of the poet continue to inspire them ; and gain him a seat with the great teachers of the world."

STUDY II.

GOD.

(CHAPTERS 1, 2, 36, 38.)

God is ādhi or first, and personal, which is indicated by the masculine termination *an*, ān, *avan* in 'pahavan, vālarivan, malar-misai-ekinan, vendhuthal-vendamai-ilan, iraivan. pori-vayil-ainthu-avitthan, thanakkuavamai-illāthān, and aravāḻi-anthanan'. Pahavan and vahutthān (377) are synonymous from pahu or vahu, meaning 'divide'. God evolves or makes the worlds out of his essence, (Ulahu-iyattiān, he who shaped the universe 1062). Vāl-arivan is a being of supreme wisdom; Malarmisai-ekinan is the deity seated or resting on the "*Spirit's folded bloom*" (compare 'pu-verukone', Thiruvasakam, Kothumbi 1 and 20.) Another reading is 'malamisai yehinān', *i.e.*, one superior to or beyond the reach of the mum-malaṣ, 'Ni-malan'. Venduthal-vendāmai-ilān or patrattavan (350) is he who has neither likes nor dislikes, neither desire nor aversion, or one to whom nought clings; iraivan, lord or king; pori-vayil-ainthavithan or one devoid of the five organs of sense and their functions; thanakku-uvamai-illathan or one who is unique or beyond compare; ara-vāḻi-anthanan, or he who is a sea of virtue and the fair and the beautiful. God is eṉkunathan or the eight-attributed, the eight attributes being evolution or creation, all-wisdom or omniscience, omnipotence or lordship, omnipresence, non-attachment absoluteness (without parts or passions), uniqueness, and virtue (grace, beauty or love). The expression also means 'ennatthakka or mathikaperum guanatthan", *i.e.*, one possessing estimable qualities. This interpretation gives no room for the learned dust of the schismatics. In chap. 36 He is Truth or Reality, 'ullathu, meiporul, sem-porul and sarpu (true support), perceivable by one who has the mystic vision, who is free from the triple tyranny of lust and wrath and error (360). Further, He is Fate or Destiny, or the apportioner of rewards and punishments for deeds, good and ill, in the past according to His fore-ordinance and first decree', *Ex pede herculem.*

God is Spirit or essence 'without parts', but has 'feet', which to worship or cling or draw near to or to praise is the fruit of learning and ensures longevity, diseaselessness, freedom from action, carking cares, and round of births, and secures heaven or infinite enjoyment. Another reading is 'matrathanāl', which seems to be more sensible and comprehensive and which signifies 'other modes do not avail.'

Thiruvalluvar is an enlightened monotheist and, obviously, an eclectic, which is manifest in his choice of epithets describing God's attributes. The student of research bent on finding out the poet's faith, will do well to apply the crucial test if any word or phrase in the invocation offends any particular creed or cult or section in the least degree. The heading, 'Kadavul Va̤lthu', for Chap. I is evidently not the poet's. 'Irai-vaṉakkam will suit it; for the heading of every chapter contains or is com-posed of words occurring in it. The commentator has played a similar trick with 'makkal-peru' and put in 'puthalvarai-peruthal' to foist his own interpretation and belief into it.

Thiruvalluvar recognises metempsychosis and realms above and regions below and angels or celestials as their denizens. He speaks of Elumai or seven worlds, or seven-fold maze of birth, *vide* 62, 107, 126, 398, 538, 835, 1278;

Vānaham 101 ; vanuraiyum theivam 50, vanore or vānat-thavar 86, 346 ; visumpulore-koman (Indra) 18 ; 'alaru' 255, 833, 919, and 'irul-serntha ulahu', 243, for the nether regions.

God is the giver of rain from heaven, without which the world (every created thing in it) is nought. It is not only food and drink in itself but makes food. In its absence cruel famine will stalk about, the ocean-wealth will decrease, no feast or offering will be made, no charity or deed of penitence will go on, nature's functions will cease, and no duty can be performed. If it be in excess, it proves destructive as inundations ; if it be moderate, it aids the ruined. It is the mainstay of agriculture, which, in its turn, is the mainstay of man. In Silapathikaram, Puhar canto, the praise of rain as a benefactor follows that of the Moon and of the Sun.

It is worthy of note that Jainism and Buddhism extolled the worship of sages but not of Gods. The Jain deity, Aruhan, or Cinendran, or lord of Wrath, is said to stand on a lotus flower, as Brahma. The expression 'eṉ-kuṉathān' is claimed by both saivites and vishnavites for their respective Godhead.

"The religion of Valluvar is a standing puzzle. He bases morality upon theology. A good or an evil action is a passport to heaven or hell. Even his invocation of the Supreme Being does not give us a clue to his religion. His theology must, therefore, be only natural theology, and his religion only natural religion. Can it be otherwise with the bard who said that 'Death is but sleep, and birth but awakening from it'" *Dr. (Pope).*

STUDY III.

GODLIKE MEN.

(CHAPTERS 3, 25—27.)

Godlike men are men who possess divine qualities and are savants, and seekers after God. They are generally called ascetics, hermits or eremites, sages, yogis, dandis, tridandis, who are absolute abrogators of self and the pleasures of the world, and whose mind will be incessantly contemplating God. They are what the moderns call supermen. Their greatness is immeasurable and untellable. The marks that distinguish them from the other renouncers of the world from indigence and destitution are restraint of the senses on a full comprehension of their operations (24-5), conquest of self and attainment of virtue (26-7), grace of character regardless of birth (30), their maledicition and benediction, as said in the scripture, being immediately effective (28), and leading the world after them (27), or the lordship of the world. "Every system has its ascetics, and self-denial is everywhere mighty". The Jain ascetics are never given to wrath, nor do they curse (25). The Christians have their Fathers, and the Mahomedans their Fakirs. Sincerity marks out the true ascetics from the sham or the hollow ones, the pure gold from the pinchbeck and the tinsel.

The true ascetic knows what will perish and what will endure. Wealth will come and go as the crowds of the dancing-hall or theatre, and it should, therefore, be well-spent (in good works) (331-3). Life is uncertain. Every day cuts off a portion of it like a bright sword (334) and that is the reason for doing good deeds at once (335). The world's greatness lies in its transitoriness, 'He was alive yesterday; to-day he is no more' (336). Though life is uncertain, our fancies are manifold and infinite (337). Body is perishable and the kinship between body and soul is short-lived and akin to that of the nest (egg) and the bird which quits it in time (338). The soul lodges in some corner of the body for a time, probably because it knows not the spacious heavenly mansion which is its house and home (340). Death is the half-brother of sleep, and birth is waking out of it, and the yogi knows it and works therefore for the cessation of these phenomena and for the mergence of the soul into the essence of God.

Renunciation (Chap. 13) implies penance or absolute privation 344, the forgetfulness of 'I and mine' 346, the abandonment of the flesh-burden 345, and the attachment to the Lord to be free from its bondage 350. Thorough renunciation, which knows no pain 341, is made in aspiration of higher pleasures 342, and it is achieved when the avenues of desire are relinquished 343.

Thorough renouncers perceive truth clearly and free from spectre-doubts that roll in cimmerian darkness on the soul 352, 353, 355, 369, have the pure mystic vision 352, think of no birth again, as it springs out of ignorance and folly 357-8 and out of desire 361, which begets grief and which should be extirpated 368, and gain eternal bliss to boot.

Those that aim at thorough renunciation do not and cannot reach the goal at once. They practise certain religious observances and virtues, positive and negative---good will (ch 25), eating no flesh (26), penance (27), non-anger (ch. 51), non-evil doing (ch. 32), non-killing (ch. 33), non-commission of fraud (ch. 29) and consistent conduct (ch. 28).

Some Benthamites seriously question the possibility of the last in a world of ceaseless compromises.

Arul or grace or charity, or tender general regard is the special characteristic of the real ascetic. All books teach this indispensable quality or virtue, 'Charity covereth a multitude of sins.' A man of charity will escape from the evil of the world and be free from vice. Experience adds its own testimony to its truth. An ungracious or graceless man cares not for higher things, can have no hope of future bliss, suffers irreparable loss, and cannot be virtuous without grace 249. A charitable man will always put himself in the place of the weaker man when he is tempted to deal harshly with him.

A man of kindly grace will abstain from flesh-eating; for the essence of grace is non-harming or killing any living being 254. The poet expresses his strong condemnation of killing game by saying that Hell devours the flesh-eaters. Neither slay nor eat the flesh of the slain. Both acts are sinful or ungracious. Buddhists preach *ahimsa* but eat the flesh of the slain, whereas the Jains eschew both 256. Killing for yagas too is to be shunned 259. He who abstains from slaying and flesh-eating is adored by the whole world.

The word *tapas*-self-mortification or more exactly self-torture is literally 'burning glow' and acquired the secondary sense of retirement into solitude in the forest, and the practice there of austerity, bodily self-mortification—not at all with the idea of atonement or penance but under the impression that self-torture of this kind would bring about magical results. Just as the sacrificer was supposed, by a sort of charm that his priests worked for him in the sacrifice, to compel the gods, and to attain ends he desired, so there was supposed to be a sort of charm in *tapas*, by which a man could, through and by himself, attain to mystic and marvellous results. The distinction seems to have been that it was rather worldly success, cattle, children, and heaven that were attained by *sacrifice*; and mystic, extraordinary, superhuman faculties that were attained by *tapas*...... It was not a mere distinction without a difference; it was a real advance in thought, when this sort of physical self-mastery, of the conquest of will over discomfort and pain, came to be placed above sacrifice".

> ' Bescorched, befrozen, lone in fearsome woods,
> Naked wihout a fire, a-fire within,
> Struggled in awful silence toward the goal',
>
> (*Buddhist India* by Rhys Davids, pp 243-5)

Real penance is not self-mortification; it is patient endurance without doing offence to others 261. It can help good men to be happy and ruin evil doers. The penitent can accomplish his wish without let or hindrance 265, and can win victory even over "Yama" or the god of death 269. Penitence helps one to possess the soul and sublimate it, 267, 268. Persons who aspire for or get such occult powers, *i.e.*, Yogis are few in the world, as many shun the penitential pains 271. An ascetic who avoids such pains is but a pretender to the life of grace 262.

An impostor to virtue is decided by the five constituents of his corporeal frame 271 and by his own conscience 272. He is compared to a steer in tiger skin 273 and to a fowler lying in ambush and shooting birds 274; to a berry of kuntri or the wild licorice shining-red outside and black at the tip 277. He is *anguis in herba*. All that glitters is not gold. The sweet lute is crooked, whereas the straight arrow is cruel and inflicts wounds 279. The shaven head and the long locks 280 and many baths in hallowed waters without a pure heart or gracious mind are useless and vain as the shadow of fame without the substance of merit or worth 272. Thus it will be seen that Thiruvalluvar condemns mere formalism and extols action in conformity with the standard of conduct set up by the average thoughtful man (sāntravan).

Be pure in spirit 281 and at heart 282 and harbour no thought of fraudulent gain which, though alluring at first, will cause undying pain in the end 283-4. Gain power by sober wisdom and not by cunning or artifice 287, and any access of power or wealth by deceit will lead to vice and, ultimately, to death or forfeiture of life and being 288-9 and to loss of celestial bliss.

It has been remarked that sincerity is the touchstone of virtue. Be true in thought 295, word 291, and deed 297, and you will be the beloved of mankind 294. Truth makes man free, pure and wise 298-9. It is a virtue incomparable 300, found by the poet from study and experience. Falsehood may have the silver lining of truth if it be beneficent and blameless 292. This couplet has been found fault with and has been the focus of ethical controversies. The poet probably means by falsehood, fictitious truth or apparent falsehood with a virtuous motive. Novels founded on human life are in the main imaginary or imaginative stories inculcating sound morals. They are not falsehoods. A tipsy man bereft of reason for the nonce hotly pursues a kinsman or a friend or a wayfarer to kill him, and asks a man who has given him shelter or refuge if he is under his roof. The latter denies it. Is he a speaker of falsehood? He saves the man without the least loss or injury to the hot pursuer. Is his action good or damnable? Should he speak the truth, a life will be unwittingly lost, without any gains to the drunken man, who, in his sane moments, will repent his senseless action and thank the averter of the sinful or wicked deed from the bottom of his heart.

The poet is no supporter of Jesuitism, nor does he blandly uphold the doctrine of 'the end justifying the means.'

True ascetics or sages are renouncers of wrath 310. It is an epigram that anger is short madness. The poet uses 'sinam' 'vehuli' and 'katham' but not the common word 'kopam'. If 'sinam' is anger or indignation indicated by the frown, 'vehuli' is burning ire or surpassing wrath expressed by outbursts or explosive acts 308-10. "Kopam papam chandālam" is a familiar saying in the form of a sorites. 'Be angry but sin not, let not the sin go down upon your anger'. The display of anger towards inferiors, equals and superiors is discriminated. The control of anger towards weaker men or inferiors is praiseworthy (301-2), and its control towards equals or superiors will proclaim impotency. Anger being the bringer of endless evils, it is better to shun it, rather forget it, regardless of the condition of its victim 303. What will be the crop of evils likely to be produced by the fiery passion ? It will deprive the face of smiles and the heart of joy 304; it will bring about his own end or ruin, 305, 308; it will slay those that approach, and will burn the raft of kindred 306. Therefore guard against anger; for a deliberate exclusion of anger from the soul will compass whatever it desires.

The negative virtues of 'not doing ill to others' and 'not slaying life.' are treated in chapters 32 and 33 respectively.

The sages or men of spotless lives hold the doctrine of *ahimsa* and condemn revenge, retribution, retaliation 311-3, and their excellence or worth lies in the rejection of all utilitarian motives, and in the embrace of *ahimsa* even to malicious foes; for the great and good men know from their studies of religious and ethical classics that it is their duty to guard others' souls from the pain which is experienced by themselves 315-6, to work no wilful woe to any soul which is immortal 317-8, and to punish wrongs by forgetting them and by conferring on the wrong-doers kindly benefits which would make them feel ashamed 314. The last, like 'forgive your enemy,' is said to be the highest ethical maxim or precept found in this masterpiece. God's mill grinds, but grinds slowly. What ill a man does before noon he has it in return in the same evening 319. Therefore the sagely thinker shuns the approach of the *thought* of evil-doing from his mind and desires freedom from its trespass 320.

What is the work of a man of virtue or of a true ascetic ? It is non-killing 321, which is the good and perfect way 324 and the sum and substance of every book of wisdom available in the world, 322. A true ascetic dreads the crime of slaughter 325 but will guard every living thing, and he will forego his own life for the sake of saving the life of others 327. He will despise all gain from slaughter 328 and will look upon slaughterers as vile folk 329 ; for he knows that slaughterers will lead loathed lives in bodies sorely pained, 330.

STUDY IV.

COURTSHIP AND MARRIAGE.

(CHAPTERS 109—123.)

Courtship is treated as furtive love (Kalavial) in seven chapters, and marriage under wedded love (Karpial) in eighteen chapters as the outcome of courtship. These chapters have for a long time been tabooed or regarded as forbidden fruit to green youngsters and to moral mortals who would not tinge their pure minds with anything savouring of carnality. The third book of Love is entitled 'Kamatthupāl', which ought to be Inpatthupāl, as 'in-pam', not 'kāmam', is one of the fourfold purushartham in Hindu literatures. This suggestion or view is endorsed and supported by stanzas 33, (35), 37, 47 and 50 against stanzas 22 and 27 only which refer to kāmam or inordinate desire, in *Tiru-Valluva-mālai*, a work assigned to the sangam age. The reader will note that *kāthalan* and *kāthali* (suitor and lover) denote the man and the woman influenced by mutual desire, and not maddened by love. Mr. Drew wrote that it could not be translated into any European language without exposing the translator to infamy. So strong and time-honoured was the prejudice against its tendency and against the poet's intention. But Tamil pandits and scholars took real delight in them or plunged deeply in them. 'To the pure all things are pure.' The third book merely gives in a succinct form the substance of the chapters on the same subject in Tolkāppiam and portrays what takes place every day in the world, between suitors and lovers, as wiving goes by destiny. Unhappily characterised as the Ghandarva marriage, this kind of meeting, mingling and mating in honour was in vogue in the Tamil land in days of yore when Tamilaham had indigenes and no aliens. With the advent of the foreigners 'with other faces and other manners', this practice fell into desuetude, for the word of honour was seldom kept by them and the marital tie, symbolised by the exchange of rings or the tying of tali, and the ceremonial sanctification became necessary and inevitable. Beauty in women and heroism in men were mutual attractions and cements of love between lovers in the palmy days of the Tamil country. Adult marriages, which were the order of the day, needed and need no legislative enactment among races that did not and do not contract infant marriages. In modern enlightened times too courtship precedes marriage in the western countries. 'Who ever loved that loved not at first sight'? wrote Christopher Marlowe, and the sentiment was endorsed by Shakespeare in his 'Merry Wives' and 'As You Like It. 'No sooner met but they looked; no sooner looked but they loved; no sooner loved but they sighed; no sooner they sighed but they asked one another the reason.' The naturalness of the consummation devoutly prayed for on both hands after repeated visits and happy communions is recommendation sufficient for the restoration of the ancient Tamil custom among the Indians of to-day of all sorts and conditions and creeds and cults, provided with proper safeguards to prevent abuse and license. The evils of early marriages and the multiplication of widows are deplorable in India above all countries.

A young man sees at a distance a charming figure and doubts if it is a goddess, a choice pea-hen, or a human being 1081. As it approaches and answers his looks, he realises a charming woman bedecked with jewels and looking more like a celestial woman 1082. Her beaming and soul-subduing eyes dart forth death-like pain 1083. Her eyes are killing, but she is simple and sweet and gracious in her form 1084. Her glance is like death's dart or resembles that of the timid fawn or is like both combined 1085. He feels that her eyebrows bent like a bow and shading the cruel beams will prove his panacea 1086. He sees her wearing on her panting bosom a silk cloth like that put on the fiery eyes of a rutting elephant 1087. He is cowed by her looks and looks a lamb, though a lion to his foes in the field of battle 1088. He finds her fair, modest and meek 1089, and her very looks are pleasing like relished honey 1090.

What are the marks of mutual love? The lover's bewitching looks pain him and heal his pain at once 1091. This couplet was a fascination to the Rev. Mr. Drew. Her furtive glance is more than half the pleasure of sexual embrace 1092. When he looks at her, she looks down, and, when he looks elsewhere, she looks at him and gently smiles 1094. Her glances are side-long looks of love 1095. Her lips disown affection, but her words are friendly 1096. They reveal love while she feigns anger and speaks harsh. Such an inconstancy is a sure sign of love 1097. It is a comforting sign that the relenting maid answers his looks and smiles softly 1098. Only lovers can make out the apparently apathetic looks of love in disguise 1099. Words are superfluous when eyes meet and confirm the mental pact 1100.

When their eyes confirm their love, the lovers are imparadised in one another's arms. The suitor gives out his sweet experiences. He says that he has derived from her all the pleasures that the five senses can afford 1101, that she was herself a remedy for the pain she gave and that the pain was delicious 1102. Nothing in heaven could equal his sweet joy when she reposed in her soft arms 1103. When he withdrew from her, his passion glowed, and, when he approached her, it cooled. Thus the love-fire was wondrous in its nature 1104. He found every variety of joy in her embrace 1105. Her shoulders were ambrosia and their touch revived his withered life 1106. Her embraces were homely ambrosia and nectar to him 1107, and were sweet and harmonious 1108, though strife, reconciliation and re-union are said to characterise lusty love 1109. His repeated embrace or intercourse made him long for more, as repeated revision of a classic discovers new meanings and yields new pleasures 1110.

The suitor descants on the beauty of her lover. To him she was more delicate or tender than the anicham flower 1111. Her eyes were flower-like and yet bewildered him. Her frame was as the tender shoot, her teeth were as pearls, her breath was as fragrance, her shoulders were bamboo-like and bow-bent, and her eyes were lances. This couplet briefly sums up all her personal charms 1113. The blue lotus drooped unable to vie with her eyes 1114. This is no hyperbole in a lover. Her waist was too tender to bear the burden of anicham flowers with stems 1115. Her face was so moon-like that the stars shot from their spheres 1116, but it did not wax and wane as the moon. It shone ever bright 1117. But for her rounded and shining face, he would love the orbed maiden ruler of the sky in the night 1118, and wish her for himself alone 1119. Her feet were so soft and delicate that the anicham flower and the swan's down were like the thorny Nerunji fruit 1120. Her voice was soft and low and her saliva was sweet as milk mixed with honey 1121. His association with her was as intimate as the bond of body and soul 1122. Her form was more iridescent than the iris and more lovely than the apple of the eye 1123. She was life to his soul when near and death when away 1124. Her charms never faded from his heart 1125. The lover felt equally with the suitor and praised him with equal warmth. She did not let his form depart from her eyes for fear that her winking would pain him and make him hide himself 1126-7. She did not dye her eyelids lest their closure shut out his image 1127. She loved him in her heart and therefore never took a hot meal lest the heat bruised it and him residing therein 1128. Her vigil was mistaken by the townsmen for his estrangement 113. It is worthy of note here that the poet has allotted an equal number of verses to the lovers to show their equal mutual devotion.

As Dame Rumour has been busy, the lovers have to abandon their reserve, and the suitor's forwardness and the lover's feminine coyness are indicated by seven verses assigned to the former and three to the latter.

The suitor makes up his mind to confess their love publicly and compass his object. In other words, he would marry her soon to put an end to the scandal. He would bestride the palmyra horse (*madal-ma*) in the night, bewail his separation from his lover, avow his union, proclaim his love and sing doleful love-ditties in her honour should she be reluctant.

The separated or unrequited suitor's *forte* lay in the horse of palm 1131, 1135, in mounting it 1132, in the open abandonment of his reserve 1133, in the sweeping away of his raft of modesty and manliness 1134, in the pangs of eventide 1135, in his keeping vigil till midnight with the thought of bestriding the palm horse 1136, and in the worth or nobility of the vexed but patient and enduring lover without recourse to the riding of the palm horse 1137.

The lover would, on her part, be chaste and tender, but her love in excess would rend the veil of modesty and shame and court publicity 1138. She would rove in highways at her wits' end and prate her love 1139, without caring for the mockery of the foolish who had no occasion to endure pangs like hers 1140.

The suitor and the lover then reflect on the good effects of the rumour set afloat, being equally determined to bring about their wedlock. So the poet has assigned them once more an equal number of verses.

The suitor says that the rumour has saved his precious life 1141, that it has made her his own 1142, that it has made explicit what was implicit 1143, that it has prevented languishment of love 1144, and that the revelation has made the love sweeter of him 1145, whereupon the lover has her say on the topic.

The lover says that the rumour has done her good, as it has spread the news of her having met the suitor once throughout the town and has taken a firm grip on the populace 1146. Though her heart languished, the town rumour has served as manure to her passion and her mother's word as irrigation to it 1147. The scandal has fed her passion and fostered it, like ghee poured on fire 1148. She would not shrink as her suitor has told her to 'fear not,' and made assurance doubly sure 1149. She would thank the townsfolk for having widely spread the rumour unsolicited and thereby hastened the desired consummation.

(Karpial) The wedlock comes to pass and the wedded pair live together and enjoy their conjugal bliss. 'But true love never runs smooth'. Occasions arise making their separation inevitable. The separated lovers have their pangs and anxious soliloquies and long for a speedy reunion.

Separation on the part of the bridegroom takes place for various reasons—for learning, money-making, waging war, peace-making, tribute-exacting, brothel-haunting, etc. At these times the bride will sit brooding on her unhappiness, ever expecting his speedy return, being unaccustomed to the sweets of æsthetic culture and education, and to civilised pastimes and pleasures.

When the bridegroom announces his departure and promises quick return, she says she cannot brook and survive it 1151. Her fear of parting saddens each embrace 1152. Her confidence in his words of living together is shaken 1153. Her trust in his assurance is no fault of hers 1154. She does not hope to live and meet him if he departs 1155, and finds it hard to expect him to be gracious ever after 1156. She had a foresign of his departure when her bracelets slipped from her wrists 1157. It is a sad thing for a woman to bid a beloved friend farewell and reside in the place in the absence of her kind kinsman 1158. The smart of love burns in hearts sundered by distance 1159. Many survive under such circumstances, bearing their distress meekly and uncomplainingly 1160. But she cannot do so. Her pain wells up as from a fountain 1161, despite the restraint of shame 1162. Love and shame weigh down her soul and balance it like a shoulder pole 1163. In the sea of love she has no trusty bark to take her to the farther shore 1164. Will not trusted friends who were April when they wooed turn December after they wedded? 1165. Do not sorrows come in battalions over a troubled soul? 1166. The midnight will be gruesome to a love-sick maiden, 1167. Sleep, which is nature's repose and balm to all, will make her keep the watches of the night 1168. When she keeps vigil all the night, the night will prove tedious and long 1169. Will not her eyes swim in tears if they can travel apace like her soul to the place of her lover's sojourn? 1170.

The eyes of the sequestered bride weep bitterly and dry and waste away and suffer pangs of irremediable pain 1171-4. The bride fancies that the eyes that had wrought her pain will have their turn 1175-6, and gloats over their aches 1177. At the thought of the separation, her eyes have no repose or rest 1178 and she has no wink of sleep as when he was with her 1179. Her eyes plainly expose the mystery of the world like the beaten tambours 1180.

The lady-lover becomes pale and ascribes her pallid hue to the bridegroom 1181-2. This sickly hue bereaves her of comeliness and shame 1183. She meditates on his words and on his worth 1184. Her pallor has taken his place 1185 and has probably waited to pounce upon her severed from his embrace 1186-7. The world casts a slur on her pining but never accuses her of being deserted 1188. Despite her pain she wishes him well 1189 and finds comfort in the world's not calling him unkind 1190.

In her solitary anguish and in the agony of suspense she consoles herself with the thought that she has secured the stoneless luscious fruit of conjugal bliss 1191 and won tender grace 1192. Only mutual lovers can make life's very joys their own 1193. Non-requital in love on either side will make both unlucky 1194, but love on both sides is good 1196. Does not the God of love know her anguish when he makes his fierce onset on her? 1197. Many brave souls endure the unkind words of their beloved 1199. A true lady is enamoured of even the melodious voice of her graceless husband I199. She who reveals her sorrow to strangers fills up the measure of her misery 1200.

She revolves many sad memories. The memory of her sexual joy is sweeter than palm-wine and always rapturous 1201-2. She takes his sneezing as the lover's thinking of her 1203. She does not forget him, but it is not known if he remembers her 1204. While he excludes her from his heart, he intrudes upon her and without shame 1205. Her life endures, she recalling her happy past 1206. The mere recollection of her past happiness burns her soul; an oblivion of it she cannot survive 1207. He never gets angry at her frequent thought of him 1208. Her precious life wastes away in pondering over his cruel oath of both being one and indissolubly knit 1209. She invokes the moon to reign in the sky that her eyes may see her departed life-partner hiding in her bosom 1210.

The lady lonely dreams and sees visions in the night. She says that the night has borne her husband's message of love 1211. If she sleeps, as she fervently wishes, she dreams that she can relate to him her long tale of woes 1212. She spends her life dreaming of her unkind lover 1213. She derives pleasure from her dream, because she sees him in it who does not visit her in waking hours 1214. She sees in her sleep pleasant dreams 1215. She assures herself that her lover will ever dwell in her heart if there be no waking hour 1216. She is puzzled with her nightly dreams when she ponders over her lover's cruelty during her waking hours 1217. In her sleep she is clasped by her lover who retreats into her heart when she wakes 1218. She who does not see her lover in her dreams will grieve for those who show no love in the daytime 1219. Her companions of the town who speak of her lover's desertion during the day do not know that he visits her in her dreams 1220.

The eventide, which afforded her pleasure in the days of their courtship and after marriage, gives her pain when her lover is away 1221. It is as cruel as her spouse 1222. Its advent has augmented her anguish and increased her sorrow 1223. It has come upon her like an alien host descending on a field of battle 1224. She hails the morning which brings her relief 1225. She never knew the torments of the eventide till her husband left her 1226. Her grief was a bud at morn, an opening flower all day, and a full-blown blossom in the evening hour 1227. The shepherd's evening pipe was to her a murderous weapon 1228. When the shades of the evening fall fast, the town will grieve 1229. The memory of the thought of her lover who has left her in quest of *fortune* kills her soul as the shades of night darken all around 1230.

Her maid observes that, while her mistress and she endure the consort's separation, the mistress's eyes weep and shun the sight of fragrant flowers 1231. Her wan and weeping eyes betray her lover's lovelessness 1232, her withered arms his unkind desertion 1233, her armlets slip and lose their charms 1234, her withered arm and slipping armlets declare his cruelty 1235. The mistress cannot bear the charge made by the maid that he is cruel to her, 236, and she speaks to her soul if it will gain any glory by making such displays and betrayals 1237. The consort far-off soliloquises likewise. He remembers how he checked her fervent embrace 1238, how her forehead turned sallow 1239, and how her eyes dimmed with sorrow 1240.

In her turn she soliloquises once more at home. She wishes her soul to suggest some cure for her malady 1241, she blames its folly 1242 and its vain pining 1243, prays to it to rid him of her eyes 1244, and consults it if she can abandon him utterly for his wan-love 1245 and for its attachment and shame 1246. She solicits her heart to give up its amour or honour 1247 and calls it a fool for its senseless longing for him 1248. She blames her soul's madness as it has her dear one in it 1249. She feels it loss of dignity and the loss of her virtue by its enshrining the heartless lover 1250. By thus soliloquising she tries to reason herself into composure but loses all her self-control and speaks of nothing but of seeing him again.

She cannot preserve her reserve for long and resolves to implore her consort's return. Love's axe breaks the door of chastity barred by the bolt of shame 1251. Love strong as death gives her no rest even at midnight 1252. However she might repress her love, it breaks out without a warning 1253. Love throws off the unassailable veil of womanly reserve 1254. The love-stricken knows no status or decorum 1250. Is it good to go after the absent lover? 1256. She will not feel shame if her lover complies with her wish 1257. His wily words unbar her heart 1258. Her heart relents and she holds him in her arms, despite her resolve not to greet him 1259. Is it possible for a melting heart to feign dislike and to stand aloof without embrace? 1260.

News runs apace that her lover will come back quick. She is anxious about it. Her eyes have lost their lustre and her scoring fingers have worn out 1261. Her shoulders will ever lose their beauty should she forget him on the hoped-for day 1262. She expects his triumphant return 1263. This couplet discloses his separation in a *state crisis,* while on a former occasion he parted from her in quest of *fortune.* She is on tiptoe for his joyous return and embrace 1264, and for the loss of her pallor 1266, and for the flight of her grief thereon 1266. She is at sixes and sevens what to do on his return to draw back or to yield herself 1267. The consort has fought long and victoriously and resolves to return home that very evening and be reunited to his wife and share the banquet with her 1268, lest she feel sorely his further delay for a single day which to her is as seven 1269, and die of a broken heart 1270.

The warrior consort returns and reads the signs of her solitary anguish in her eyes 1271, notwithstanding her modest reserve and restraint 1272 of her inexpressive thought in her gleams 1273, of her secret budding in her smiles 1274, and of her wiles medicinal to his grief 1275. Her turn comes and she reads the signs of his unavoidable separation once more 1270 in her armlets getting loose 1277. His departure took place on the preceding day, but his sallow complexion proclaimed his long absence 1278. Her companion reads the signs of her mistress's love-sickness in her tender arms and sliding armlets, in her feet 1279 and in her eye 1280, and feels that woman's most womanly service is to pray for relief by her ocular entreaty.

The thought of the lover's return and the sight of him delight her heart 1281; for perfect love casts out the least distrust 1282. She longs to see him and give ease to her heavy heart 1283. Though prepared for cool disdain, her heart melted at his sight 1284 and it could not see any fault in him 1285, though in his absence she saw in him nothing but faults 1286. She could not hold out her feigned anger long, as surely as the plungers in floods dreaming of their rescue 1287. Her consort was traitorous to his love and shameless as a drunkard 1288. The rapture on sexual love is known to few 1289. Her angry eyes overpowered by love proved her excessive tenderness 1290.

The lady now expostulates with herself and feels sorry that her soul cannot contain itself 1291, but goes to him 1292, because of its helplessness, as they say 'the ruined have no friends,' 1293. To submit after counselling to show offended pride will unbecome her soul 1294. Her heart endures unceasing pain at the fear of its loss after its present gain 1295. Her solitary reflection makes her bemoan his cruelty 1296. Caught in the clutches of her foolish heart, she has hardened herself to shame 1297. Her heart feels it disgraceful to contemn him as it clings to life in utter selfishness 1298. She has none but her heart to aid her in her moments of grief 1299. When her heart turns a stranger to her, how can aliens be expected to behave like kinsmen? 1300.

She still soliloquises. She pouts to prove his sore distress 1301, but she will not pout long lest the seasoning salt prove bitter in its excess 1302. It is the duty of a consort to beguile his pouting lover 1303 and to embrace her in order to cut short her agony 1304. The wifely petulance is looked upon as a grace even by good and worthy men 1305. Love without short-lived strife is like a green fruit, and love without hatred is like a fruit too matured or ripe 1306. Feigned dislike doubts embrace, speedy or tardy 1307. A lover's grief is fruitless when no wife is there to appreciate it 1308. Temporary coolness with a lover is akin to water in the cooling shade 1309. It will be uxorious to love her, persisting and perverse in her quarrel 1310.

When the husband returns from a prostitute's embrace, the chaste wife shrinks from embracing him 1311. Here the poet alludes to the *third* reason for separation on the part of the husband. The sulking lover shows her refined petulance by asking her consort if he sneezed expecting her to say long life to him 1312. When the consort wears flowers, it is womanly jealousy that forces her to know the reason why 1313. When he declares his love for her above all, her jealousy provokes her to question him 'What all, what all,' When he says that he will not quit her in this life or while he is here, she is afraid that he will abandon her there *i e.*, in the next 1315. At his words that every day he remembered her charms, she unclasped her arms and would not embrace him 1316. She blessed him when he sneezed, but suddenly changed her mind and asked him in jealousy if he did not sneeze thinking of some other woman 1317. When he suppressed his sneezing next time, she was in tears and told him that he hid his thoughts from her 1318. When he tried to soothe and coax her with a view to calm her jealous soul, she said that it proved wondrous kindness and cajolery to other womenfolk 1319. When he sat in silent meditation and gazed at her charming figure, she asked him whose form he saw in her and mused over 1320. Thus it will be seen that a lady in sulks finds a pretext, however light, for worrying her lover with inconsequential tattle.

Oodal is temporary variance. The lady finds nothing blameable in her consort, but love provokes jealousy 1321. Pain increases when affection droops 1322. Hearts in sweet concord enjoy divine bliss in womanly coyness 1323. Temporary variance binds the love-tie closer, but prolonged quarrel tends to rend it 1324. The consort replies that estrangement for a time has its special charms 1325 and that it is sweeter in love than union (as digestion is more important than eating) 1326. He who succumbs in lover's quarrels proves a victor in the joy of reunion 1327. Reunion proves sweeter with the piquant grace lent to it by feigned dislike 1328. The prolongation of night is invoked by the consort to have time to plead on and wipe off aversion from her heart 1329. A brief quarrel adds zest to love and a hearty embrace will prove the roof and crown of it all.

The substance of the third book on love has been reproduced in this Study at length with a purpose. It is to demonstrate to the reader how innocuous it is to him, what knowledge of human nature and of the psychology of the sexes it imparts to him, for lack of which many a married couple daily hurls itself into 'the vortex of irretrievable ruin and how unjust is the taboo pronounced against it by savants and sages.' Bacon observes "Nuptial love maketh mankind; friendly love perfecteth it; but wanton love corrupteth and embaseth it."

STUDY V.

MAN AND WIFE

(CHAPTERS 4 to 24, 91—2, 103.)

How laconic is the Victorian laureate's dictum put in the mouth of a happy husband, describing the three successive stages of a woman's life—'my bride, my wife, my life.' In the last Study it was seen how the first stage glided into the second, and in this will be studied the justification for the third, *i.e.*, the virtues and amenities of a partner for life. The relationship between a husband and a wife and their offices in life in the medieval ages are portrayed by Lord Tennyson in these verses:

> " This is fixt
> As are the roots of earth and base of all;
> Man for the field and woman for the hearth;
> Man with the head and woman with the heart;
> Man to command and woman to obey;
> All else confusion * * * *
> The bearing and the training of the child
> Is woman's wisdom."

Thiruvalluvar and his sweetheart Vasuki are said to have lived as model man and wife. The poet's eulogy on the death of his dear enumerates her virtues—an expert cuisinier, loving and obedient, a masseuse, a late sleeper and an early riser. Nothing is said in it about her culture and education.

Rev. Dr. Pope has given a rapid summary of the duties of man and wife as follows. "The ideal householder leads on earth a consecrated life (50) not unmindful of any duty to the living or to the departed (42). His wife, the glory of his house, is modest and frugal, adores her husband, guards herself and is the guardian of his house's fame chap vi. His children are the choicest treasures; their babbling voices are his music; he feasts with the gods when he eats the rice their tiny fingers have played with; and his one aim is to make them worthier than himself vii. Affection is the very life of his soul; of all his virtues, the first and greatest. The sum and source of them all is love viii. His house is open to every guest, whom he welcomes with smiling face and pleasant word and with whom he shares his meal ix. Courteous in speech, grateful for every kindness xi, just in all his dealings xii, master of himself in perfect self-control xiii, strict in the performance of every assigned duty xiv, pure xv, patient and forbearing xvi, with a heart free from envy xvii, moderate in desires xviii, speaking no evil of others xix, refraining from unprofitable words xx, dreading the touch of evil xxi, diligent in the discharge of all the duties of his position xxii, and liberal in his benefactions xxiii, he is one whom all unite to praise xxiv".

In the Introductory chapter on 'arram' or righteousness and merit or charity and charitable acts, virtue yields fame and well-being. To be spotless in mind is more than alms-giving; to be free from envy, wrath, lust, ill words is the soul's grace and accomplishment 34, 35. Be good to-day and at once 36; for life is uncertain, and do good every day lest you miss your aim. The practice of virtue in this life will help you to be happy and to terminate the round of births. The man borne in a litter and its bearers discriminate the virtuous man from the rest of the world 37.

A great poet has said that the big coach of life will not move but will stand still if man and wife do not pull on together and well. The virtues of blameless domestic life 49, are the fostering of father, mother, and guru 41, the other-worldly, the unowned dead 42, the caring of the southerners (Tamils), the worship of their deity (Siva), the cherishing of their guests, kindred and self 43, hospitality or dividing one's hard-earned bread with others 44, good behaviour, love 45, and conformity to the ways of the world 50, *i.e.*, its best men.

Love is the basis of domestic life. The selfish are loveless ; the altruistic are loving to the bone 72. The life of love is the fruit of the union of body and soul 73. Love exhibits itself in tiny tear drops, however suppressed 71. Love begets yearning and true friendship 74. It produces earthly felicity and heavenly bliss 75. It fosters virtue and is an aid to curb vice 76. Life without love is akin to sapless trees in barren soil bearing flowers 77. The possession of soul devoid of love in a perfect body is of no use, and the body is the seat of life when love resides within 80. The guardian genius of virtue oppresses loveless beings, as the blazing sun does the boneless creatures 77.

What are the virtues of a good wife? A wife is a helpmate if she respects self and practises frugality 51. Chastity is woman's treasure 54 and her safest guard 57 and gains her divine bliss 58, and a worthy wife, who is luck in the house 53, guards herself, cares for the comfort of her husband and for the fame of the family, governs her tongue and is always brisk and alive 56. Such a wife is a blessing to the husband 60, and spouses without a good name scandalise the lordly lions of their husbands 49.

The begetting of blessed children is the goodly ornament of an excellent wife 60. Children must be virtuous, wise, and worthy, and are a fortune to their parents 61-3 who hold dear as ambrosia the food played with by them 64, to whom their touch is sweet, and their voice sweet music, sweeter than the pipe and the lute esteemed by the childless 65, 66. · The duty of the father is to educate the children better than himself and make them shine in witenagemots 67 ; the mother feels intense joy when the world praises the wisdom of her children 69, and the duty of the son is to make men say that he should have been begotten by his father after great penance 70. Verse 51 gives the author's own experience, ' we know not any greater gain of all that men acquire ', and verse 52 the author's belief ' in the sevenfold maze of births.' Chapter vii speaks of parents and children, not exclusively of sons, and its proper heading should, therefore, be ' makkal peru ' or ' the begetting of children,' rather than ' puthalvarai-peruthal '.

Hospitality is a domestic virtue ; it is the virtue par excellence of a vellala, ' vellalan enpan virunthirukka unnathan ' (a vellala will never eat without feeding his guest.) Guests ought to be received with courtesy 81, with kindliness 83, and with a smiling face 84, for they will be tender-hearted and delicate and shrink as the anicha flower which withers away at the mere touch 90. Where the great sacrifice (velvi) prevails will be the habitat of fortune 84 and a full granary 83. A good host is he who tends the guest at home and expects the coming one 86 and he who turns away from them is penury itself, despite his riches, and is folly incarnate 89. The measure of true hospitality is the worth of the guest treated 87.

While kind words x, Gratitude xi, Impartiality xii, Self-restraint xiii, Decorum, Forbearance xvi, Duty xxii, Gift xxiii, are virtues, adultery xv, coveting xviii, back-biting xix, vain words xx, evil deeds xxi, are sins, and they and other kindred topics will be trested in the study entitled " Virtues and Vices ".

Man and Wife, if they be true to themselves, will achieve renown 238, and they themselves are to blame and will be looked on as dead if they do not live without reproach 240.

Chapter 91 deals with uxors who sell their souls to the demon of wifely love 901. A wealthy uxor will reap shame 902, as a submissive or timid or quaking uxor 903-6, however god-like or majestic he seems. An obedient uxor cannot help his friends in need 908 or perform charitable acts 909, nor can he enjoy pleasure 910. Modest womanhood will be more dignified and preferred to uxorious manliness 907.

Wanton women are the bane of society. They are charming and beautiful and wear choice ornaments and jewels, speak pleasant words 911, 913, 914, display wheedling arts 916, feign embrace 91 for wealth, and possess double minds 920, and these Dalilas or luring demonesses 918 will be sought only by the thoughtless, by the unwise and graceless 915, by the unrighteous 917, by the abject 919, and by the unlucky 920. As they are living and moving hells, they who seek delight in their society are said to inarm some strange corpse in a darkened room 913.

Virtuous husbands will neither be uxorious nor caught in the tangled net of mercenary women, and good wives will never lend themselves to the loss of dignity, worth or reputation of their spouses.

This Study will close with chapter 103, which describes the way of maintaining the family. Those who will rear up the race, build the fame of the family and augment the praise of the house must be men of strong resolution and steady hand 1021, of full knowledge and daring deed 1022, or fearless heroism 1027, of activity without supineness and without looking for the season or the fit opportunity 1028 and of strong intellectual powers 1026. Such men are truly great whom no sorrow or trouble can daunt, whom the world will embrace and whom it will claim as kindred 1025.

That Tiruvalluvar's view of sex-relationship has not risen above the medieval standard is patent. Its perfect ideal of the realisation of a manly womanliness and a womanly manliness is presented in the following lines by the same master-poet of the Victorian Era whose verses on the ideal of the Middle Ages have preluded this Study.

> " In the long years liker must they grow ;
> The man be more of woman, she of man ;
> He gain in sweetness and in moral height,
> She mental breadth, nor fail in childward care,
> Nor lose the childlike in the larger mind ;
> Till at the last she set herself to man.
> Like perfect music unto noble words ;
> And so these twain, upon the skirts of Time
> Sit side by side, full summ'd in all their powers,
> Dispensing harvest, sowing the To-be,
> Self-reverent each and reverencing each,
> Distinct in individualities,
> But like each other ev'n as those who love,
> Then comes the statelier Eden back to men :
> Then reign the world's great bridals chaste and calm :
> Then springs the crowning race of humankind."

STUDY VI.

VIRTUES AND VICES.

(CHAPTERS 11-14, 17-9, 21-22, 58-62, 79-83, 93, 94, 96-9, 101, 105-108.)

Many are the virtues and vices prevalent in human society which every man ought to acquire or rid himself of. The ascetic virtue based on grace has been treated under Godlike men, Study III. Here we speak of the domestic virtue based on affection and of virtues and vices in general. Soft speech, gratitude, impartiality, self-restraint, decorum, forbearance, duty, dower, benignity, energy, manly effort, hopefulness, friendship, nobility, honour, greatness, perfectness, courtesy, sense of shame, are some of the virtues, and baseness, mendicancy, poverty, gaming, tipsiness, sloth, envying, backbiting, coveting, gossiping, and adultery are some of the vices discussed in this universal moral Code. Virtue and Vice have been defined by the poet in couplet 40 thus;

> " *Virtue* sums the things that should be done ;
> *Vice* sums the things that man should shun".

A ***kind word*** is more than a coronet. It should spring up from the fountain of sincerity and should be accompanied by a beaming smile and a loving eye and humility 92, 94, 95. It works out vice and fosters virtue. When it is free from meanness, it affords pleasure 98, 99, here and otherwhere, and to prefer the use of bitter words is to make a choice of the sour unripe fruit while the sweet ripe one is ready to hand 100. 'A soft answer turneth away wrath'.

Gratitude for favours received, unsolicited and in time and without expectation of return is worth more than earth and heaven 101-3, and will be deemed high by the wise and the thoughtful 104. Favour is measured not by its quantity but by the worth of the receiver 105 and timely aid by virtuous men deserves to be remembered through the sevenfold births 107. It is good to remember any good done to us; but it is better to forget the evil 108. The remembrance of a past good action will erase the deadliest injury done at present 109. Surely the ungrateful will never escape ruin 110. 'Besotted base ingratitude,' says Milton. 'Blow, blow, thou winter wind, Thou art not so base as man's ingratitude' says Shakespeare.

Impartiality (justice) is to give each man his due 111, and an impartial man will fare well 112. The golden mean is the rule of virtue and an unswerving mind is an ornament of the virtuous 115. To be partial and to gain by partiality are evil ways and are sure to work ruin 113, 116. A man's partiality or otherwise can be gauged by his offspring or by the result of his actions 114. Impartiality or an equitable soul is like a balance-rod 118, and the word of righteousness is the outcome of the soul being in the right 119. The test of impartiality is disinterestedness or altruism 120. Even-handed justice is what is meant by impartiality. Justice, pure and simple, is a divine attribute, and, in the words of the lady lawyer Portia, 'in the course of justice none can have salvation,' unless it be tempered with mercy, or unless mercy seasons justice.'

Self-control is a power that leads to sovereign sway 123 and is therefore a precious treasure of the soul 121-2. A man of self-control will attain high glory, as high as the mountain summit 124. Humility to all comes of self-control and is fortune's diadem 125. Self-control implies the restraint of the five senses like the tortoise 126, and the government of the tongue 127 ; for an evil word will ever be the parent of evil 128, and its effect will be permanent, ineraseable, and unforgettable 129. The restraint of wrath is the path to virtue 130.

Decorum is a virtue and is more precious than life 131. It must be learnt and kept 132, as it is true nobility on earth 133. Indecorum proves base birth and loses the birthright of dignity irretrievably 134-5. The breach of decorum brings on disgrace 136 and undeserved censure 137 and eternal sorrow 138. A decorous man will never speak an ill-word even unwittingly 139 and knows how to dwell in harmony with the world 140. Men's evil manners live in brass while their good manners which are the fruit of culture and of a noble mind, are writ in water or passed over by the bustling world.

Patience and forbearance are noble qualities. A man should be as patient as the mother earth is even to the digger. 'To err is human, to forgive is divine.' Forgive and forget is a good maxim to hold to 152. To bear with folly is a mighty act 153. It must be kept up as honour 154, and forbearance is prized as precious gold 155 and merits eternal praise 156. It is noble patience to grieve for the sin of others and to restrain one's passion 157. A patient forbearer of transgression is a true ascetic and will gain the foremost place in the world 160. Patience smiles at grief. In advising a man to forget others' trespasses, St. Valluvar really transcends Jesus, 'who only wants to forgive them' (Pope). In advising to forget trespasses our author is only in the positive degree ; in asking to deal righteously with the wrong-doer he is in the comparative degree ; in exhorting to do kindly benefits and pass over the evil done he is surely in the superlative degree.

Duty, duty clear of recompense, clear of consequences, is likened to rain 211. It is a source of wealth to be used for beneficence to others 212 and there is nothing on earth or heaven equal to it 213. It is one's duty to know the grace of life 214. The riches of dutiful men will serve mankind like the full lake amidst a village and like the fruit-bearing tree therein 215-6, and like the tree of the healing balm 217. The poverty of a duteous man is the lack of opportunity to be kind 218, and to do good deeds 219. Duty should be fulfilled at any cost or risk, even by selling oneself 220. Fear God and keep His commandments—this is 'the whole duty of man' says the Bible.

Dower or *gift* to needy men is real giving, without thought of recompense 221. It is a great virtue though the heavens fall 222. 'Nay' never comes out of a noble man's lips 223. Gifts must be made personally 224 ; in the form of food to relieve the pangs of hunger, food which a man shares with the hungry 227. The feeder of the hungry will have no hunger-malady. One who hoards up wealth without beneficence loses it and has no pleasure 228. Miserliness is worse than mendicancy 229 and worse than death 230.

True *benignity* dwells in royal souls, and the world goes on due to its presence 571. It is essential to the eye as a song to the sounding chord 573 and as an ornament of grace to it 575. The kind eye is ever bright 574. The graceless eye is like the tree fixed in the earth 576 and is blind 577. The benignant smiler makes the world his own 578. It is great benignity to smile with kindly face and to possess the soul with long patience 579 even when one is vexed, and to drink poison knowingly when it is administered 580.

The possession of virtuous *energy* is a test of self-control 591. Energy gives mind wealth and worth 592 and never despairs 593 but is favoured by fortune 594. It imparts and measures dignity 595 and engenders a high ideal, though now and then thwarted by fate 596. It quails not in crisis like the dignified elephant amid showers of arrows 597. The unenergetic man can have no influence on men 598. He resembles the huge tusked elephant trembling before a small fierce-looking tiger 599. Energy is to man real excellence and the lack of it makes him a walking tree 600.

Manly effort gives prevailing power 611 and will never leave work undone 612. By it alone others can be helped 613. Beneficent intent without manly or strenuous effort is like the sword-holding by a sexless being 614. Manly effort cuts off kinsmen's griefs and makes them mighty 615. It makes one's fortune bright 616, and the lack of it brings misfortune 617 and foul disgrace, though fate be averse to it 618. It will gain its sure reward, though thwarted by divine fate 619 and have the upper hand of it if it be undismayed and unfailing 620.

Optimism is good, particularly in crises. A hopeful heart seldom worries itself or is gloomy. Nothing has equal power with it to dispel grief or to roll back the Atlantic of sorrow 622-5. It will not bemoan loss 626 either from the sense of man's frame being sorrow's targe or from an implicit faith in the divine governance of the world 627-8. He whom joys do not affect is not affected by sorrow 629. He who can derive pleasure from pain or take pain as pleasure will be blessed 630.

True friendship (kenmai, thodarpu) is a sure defence ; it waxes like the crescent moon and grows sweeter day by day

781-3. It sharply reproves when the friend swerves from the path of righteousness or duty 784. It brings kindred hearts together though sundered by distance, without constant association and token of affection 785. It is not facial smile but the smile of the heart 786 that saves one from ruin, keeps him in the way of virtue and weeps with the suffering friend 787. It will stay the coming grief like the hand that instinctively pulls up the slipping vesture 788.- A friend in need is a friend indeed 789. Friendship blazing forth its intimacy and worth is despicable 790. Friendship formed without due or prolonged investigation or trial will give pain 791-2. The marks of good friendship are temper, descent, knowledge of defects and flawless associations 793. Once friendship is formed after due investigation and trial, it must be kept up or grappled with hoops of steel. *Noble friendship* shrinks from guilt with shame 794. True friendship, as already pointed out, reproves and moves repentance in a friend going astray 795, and continues firm even in his ruin 796. It does not forsake in times of grief, though it puts away fools 797-8 and renounces the wicked while it clings to the spotless 800. It is not true friendship but torture in life to drop or desert a sinking friend 799. Ancient friendship does not stand on stilts 801 but claims freedom, its sweet savour 802. *Unresponsive friendship* is fruitless 803, but responsive friendship takes the unbidden kindly deed in good part 804. Familiarity must not breed contempt or distress of mind by folly or carelessness; it must be within bounds 805-6. *Old loving friendship* overlooks betrayals 807, and offences 808. An old and faithful friendship is commended by the world 809 and is wished good even by ill-wishers 810. The fruits of friendship are said to be peace in the affection (cutting away griefs in halves), support of the judgment (maketh daylight in the understanding) and aid and bearing a part in all actions and on all occasions; for a friend is another himself.

Unreal friendship is formal, friendship without the consenting mind. It would always have an axe to grind 821. *Apparent* friendship will be like the Vicar of Bray changing with the tides and times 822. *Heart-felt* friendship, which is a cement of the soul, is never a virtue of the ignoble 823. One may smile and smile and be a villain. *Dissembling* friendship is villainous 824. Friendship where hearts are wide apart cannot be true 825. Goodly words spoken in a friendly tone betray the hollow heart 826. Pliant speech without a pliant heart will be as deadly as a pliant bow 827. *Hypocritical* friendship weeps with a dagger at heart or concealed in the palm of the hand 828. It is *murderous* friendship to praise a man to his face and cheer him up before slaying him 829. To such friends one may do like for like 830.

Evil friendship should not be allowed to continue so long as the heart is alien. *Trencher* friends and *summer* friends are to be abhorred as parasites. They swarm in prosperity and vanish in adversity 811-2. Calculators in friendship are of the marauding kidney 813. Aloofness from such is preferable to being with them in friendship's guise 814. They are evil friends who fail you in dangers 815. The wise man's hate is preferable to the fool's intimacy 816 or to that of the vain laughers 817. The succour of a friend without love ought to be eschewed 818. It is better to eschew intimacy even in dreams with men who profess kindness but do evil 819 and who speak well at home and slander in mote-halls 820. The poet has devoted *five whole chapters* to friendship and its simulacra and given the marks of true friendship with a view to help to distinguish and discriminate and sift the wheat from the tares and chaff. Friendship is a sheltering tree and knows no cold medium, as the poet says, if it is true. It is cut-throatism to feign it and cynicism to regard it as a shade that follows wealth or fame and leaves the wretch to weep. Though friendship has been called 'glorified love', it is not and can never be love.

Nobility is a virtue. It is characterised by its instinctive sense of right and wrong 951, by its virtuous deed, truthful word, chastened thought 952 and by its gift, smiling countenance, soft speech and courtesy at all times 952. It will never stoop to do sin and blind the soul with clay 954, whatever the temptations. It will never fail in its ancestral grace, though means may be lacking to do charity 955. It will ever try to keep up the fame and prestige of its ancestry 956. Its faults will be conspicuous in the world's eye as spots in the sun 957. Its ancestry will be seriously doubted if it be devoid of love 958. Soft speech, virtuous shame and true reverence are the sure outward tests of true nobility 959-60.

The poet has said 'act well your part, there all the honour lies'. A man of *honour* will reject soul-staining 961 or inglorious acts 962, but will be humble and modest 963 in his prosperity. Loss of honour is loss of rank and despicable as the fallen hairs of the head 964. Meanness, slight as abrus (Kuntri), is a mark of dishonour however high the status 965. To follow scorners and do thelr bidding is dishonourable, being an act destitute of praise and heavenly attainment 966. It is better to perish under the circumstances 967. It is love of the body to survive the loss of honour 968. Death will be preferable to dishonour like the wild ox losing a single tuft of hair from its body 969 ; and he who prefers death to dishonour, like Brutus, will live for ever in honour in the heart of the world. 'Mine honour' says Norfolk in *Richard II* 'is my life, both grow in one, Take honour from me and my life is done.'

Wherein lies true *greatness ?* Worth makes the man. It depends on the energy of the mind, on the quality of his work and not on birth either high or low 971-3. Greatness is like virgin purity to be true to self 974. A great man does rare deeds in a perfect manner and all men will enroll themselves as votaries 976. He will never be haughty or insolent nor will he indulge in hyperbolic self-praise 977-8. A mean man will be conceited, fond of display, vain, and ready to proclaim others' faults, 979-80.

Perfectness or *perfect goodness* lies in walking virtues' perfect way. Every dutiful man is a good man, as goodness transcends or is above all carnal delights 981-2. Goodness is tested by inward excellence, and its five props are love, modesty, beneficence, benignity, and truth 983. Goodness hates scandal, loves submission, preserves perfect equilibrium of mind at defeat, seldom thinks of retaliation to evil-doers, and does not fret at the lack of every earthly good. It will continue unimpaired in the world's cataclysm, which is generally the outcome of its decrease in the world. 'Santanmai' will kill the foeman's rage and keep the world in its swing 984-90.

Courtesy is not mere politeness : it comprises easy accessibility to all, benevolence, noble dignity, and dispensing benefits (equity and charity) 991, 2, 4. Physically or constitutionally all men may agree, but they differ in the endowment of attractive qualities 993. Courteous men are above all reproach ; but for them, the world will go to wreck and ruin 995-6. Discourteous men, though sharp and witty, are mere blocks of wood 997. It is the pink of courtesy founded on humility and generosity that will not fail itself towards doers of unfriendly acts and wrongs 998. It is discourtesy not to know how to smile in kindly mirth 999. The wealth of a discourteous or churlish person will be as sour as good milk poured in a filthy vessel 1000. The heart of courtesy is the home of high-erected thoughts, as Sir Philip Sidney says.

Shame or *sense of shame* is manifested in shrinking from every-evil deed 1011 ; it is a mark of excellence 1012. It is the habit of virtue 1013 and an ornament to men of dignity 1014 while stately pride is a piteous thing. It arises from the consciousness of one's own guilt or of that of others 1015. It is a hedge that protects the world's charms to lofty souls 1016. It will never be sacrificed to save life 1017. Virtue will disclaim one who lacks the sense of shame 1018, and shamelessness will consume every good 1019. Shameless beings are wooden puppets aping life's functions 1020. Lord Churchill says that 'those who fear not guilt yet start at shame.'

The worst of vices is *baseness*. Base men are but men in form and shape, and the poet says he has not seen their counterpart in creation. Their freedom from anxiety makes them think they are superior to grateful hearts 1072. In their freedom to do what they list they resemble the gods, 1073. They exult and smile over their superiority to men of vile conduct 1074. They act from fear or hope of gain 1075 and disclose secrets aloud as drum-beats 1076. They will give only to the breakers of their jaws with clenched fists 1077, or to their torturers like the sugarcane 1078. They try to trace or detect some flaw when they see their neighbours well-fed and clad 1079. They sell themselves outright in times of grief 1080.

Two chapters deal with *mendicancy and the dread of it.* It is graceful, says the poet, to ask alms of proper persons who never deny and to receive it without annoyance 1052-3. It is sinful to deny alms to the deserving 1051. Mendicancy is resorted to, because there are men ready to give 1055. The ready-givers never fall a prey to poverty 1056. Mendicants are joyous when they are given without harsh words 1057. Without mendicants men will be like wooden puppets devoid of discretion and free-will 1058, or of generous impulses 1059. Mendicants should never get angry when their asking is not complied with 1060. It is a noble thing not to live by alms 1061, as it cannot be the intention of the maker of the world that men should go a-begging 1062 and relieve their poverty thereby 1063. It is a noble resolve never to go a-begging even in the direst need 1064. A mess of pottage won by self-labour will be sweeter than a rich repast given gratis 1065. Begging water even for a cow is vile to the tongue 1066. Beggars must make it a point not to beg of habitual deniers 1067; for the frail bark of beggary will be wrecked on the rock of denial 1068. The thought of mendicancy will melt any heart, but stern repulse will break it 1069. Denial pains a beggar to death; if so, where will the spirit of the refuser take refuge? 1070.

The West looks upon *poverty* as a crime and the East as a sin or as a vice, for an industrious poor man will keep the wolf from the door, at least, keep his body and soul together. Utter poverty (nalkuravu, nirappu) is unique in the pain it causes 1041. As it gives pain, it drives away bliss, here or otherwhere 1042. Poverty brings on oblivion and augments sorrows 1043-4; its good sense and effective expression are lost on the world 1045-6; it is loathsome even to the mother 1047, and its recurrence is dreaded 1048; it knows no repose and burns hotter than fire 1049, and, in the absence of renunciation, it is Yama to the neighbour's salt and gruel. According to the poet Gray 'Chill penury represt their noble rage and froze the genial current of their soul.' So the prayer runs 'give me neither poverty nor riches.' But Dr. Johnson says 'This mournful truth is everywhere confessed, 'slow rises worth by poverty depressed' and our poet himself tells us elsewhere that severe self-denial, like gold in a crucible, needs to be heated to be purified.

Gaming or *gambling* and *toddy* or intoxicant *drinking* are condemned as baneful vices. Avoid gambling then, the dice, the play and the art; for it is seductive. One ga in allures to a thousand losses. It is like a bait of the fish 931-2. It will deprive a gamester of his wealth and his other resources and reputation and bring on endless miseries 933-7. Gambling is a synonym or alias of misfortune 936. It bends the soul to falsehood 938. A lover of gambling loses his clothes, wealth, food, praise and learning 939. Losses cannot deter a gambler's heart which is ever in the play 940. The vice kindred to it is tipsiness due to drinking intoxicants. Toddy drinking, it is said, relieves physical pain. This vice of cold climates is costly; it destroys public esteem, reverence and glory 921-2, It brings sorrow to the mother 923, shame 924, self-oblivion 925, and death-like poison 926. A drunkard is the townsmen's jest and laughing stock 927, for tipsiness opens up the secrets buried in the heart as in a Pandora's box 928. Wine is the enemy put in the mouth to steal away the brains. It is vain effort to reason a drunkard into sobriety, as to try to find a man who has found a wavery grave with a lantern in hand 929. If a man getting sober after quaffing the inebriating beverage sees a tipsy man, the still small voice within him will surely recall to him his own folly in his reveries 930.

Moderation is medicine. Use a little wine for thy stomach's sake. A hard day-labourer drinks to take off the pain of his body and an ease-loving man takes to dice to while away his heavy hour. When the former drinks like a sponge and does it daily many times and in excess, he ruins his health, his economy, his household, his name and fame. Similarly the dice-man addicted to the game loses all and sells even his soul. The chess play is very popular now with educated men who have recourse to it for change and recreation, to take off the tediousness of the dull professional routine and to refresh the jaded spirits after the day's hard work though the game is taxing to the brain and consumes time. The little pleasure of the game is to view it from afar and not to get into the thick of it and bet heavily as do princes and lords of lands vast and wide. It is heinous and ruinous to a gamester,

> " Whose game is empires, and whose stakes are thrones.
> Whose table earth—whose dice are human bones."

In his Vedic India, pp. 375-7 writes Z. A. Ragozin as follows:

'The leading vices of the Aryan race have always been drinking and gambling. The Rig Veda bears ample witness to both: the materialistic symbolism of soma worship greatly helped to confirm, almost inculcate, the former by the stress it laid on the supposed divine (fiery) element in the sacred intoxicant. Gambling in the form of dice is almost frequently alluded to. But we would scarcely expect, at so early a date, a portrayal of a gambler's career, so modern, if we may say so, alive with actuality, as that given in the so-called hymn X 34. It is the gambler who speaks in his own person and no *habitue* of Monte Carlo could lay bare more remorseful and helpless self-condemnation in the ruthless grip of the enthralling passion, or depict more graphically its disastrous effects on home and family. 'They are like fish-hooks that pierce the flesh ; deceivers that burn and torture. After a brief run of luck, they ruin the winner; yet are they to the gambler sweet as honey.' That the vice of gambling should breed the worse vice of cheating at play stands to reason. Accordingly, we find it mentioned in the Rig Veda with a frequency and familiarity which shows the practice to have been a common one, though accounted very heinous.'

Idleness or *sloth* (madi) compasses the ruin of an idler's name and fame ; indolence kills the family dignity and prestige 601-2. It works mischief like a silly elf 603. Under its shade folly thrives 604. Like delay, oblivion and sleep, the pleasure-boat of indolence leads to wreck and ruin 605. The sluggard gains no good whatever his store 606. He will be reproved, rebuked and reproached by the world and held in contempt 607. He will become the slave of his foe 608. But he who casts off indolence saves himself from perdition 609 and holds sway over the world's mind 610.

Envy, called the 'evil eye' and 'witch craft,' is a degrading vice of the mind and the worst curse of man ; it feels one's fate, will own nothing in the way of food or dress, consigns the soul to fiery pain and will gain no felicity. It is embodied evil and incomparable bane and the envious man's increase of joy will engage thoughtful minds 161-70. James Thompson has 'Base envy withers at another's joy and hates that excellence it cannot reach', and Pope says 'Envy will pursue merit as its shade, but, like a shadow, proves the substance true". Public envy is called *invidia* or discontentment and "the envious man soweth tares amongst the wheat by night". Dr. Bain defines envy as "the feeling of inferiority with a malevolent sentiment towards the rival." According to Christopher Marlowe the cause of *covetousness* is excess of wealth

Covetousness is a sin which opens the door to evil 171. Lust of gain brings about retribution 172. It is base desire and evil aspiration 173. It has sordid vision of others' goods 174. It turns to folly and is an abuse of learning 175. In its desire of wealth it does wrong deeds and loses all grace 176. Greed never yields good fruit 177. The desire to make another's riches one's own brings about the decline of prosperity 178, and bids good-bye to good fortune 179, and is the cause of fatal ill 180.

Backbiting, secret calumny, slander, defaming behind the back, all are synonymous terms. A backbiter is a scorner of virtue, though a smiler and a panegyrist in one's presence, and is the meanest of men 'without a soul of goodness' 181-5. He takes delight in expatiating on his neighbour's sins 186, severs hearts by his words and cuts off friends 187, defames good names 188, and is a burden and a load even to the patient mother Earth 189. He will not slander another if he sees his own faults as his neighbours' 190. Shakespeare says " Be thou as chaste as ice, as pure as snow, thou shalt not escape calumny ", and thereby demonstrates that no man or woman, however good or worthy, can be free from the serpent-bites and the adder-stings of backbiters.

Gossip is idle talk or tittle-tattle or talk without sense, which is despised by all, and is more offensive 191-2. It proclaims the speaker's unwisdom or folly and delights none 193-4. Gossip by the wise or the worthy forfeits fame and worth 195-7. A gossiper is no man; he is the chaff of humanity 196. Saints, sages, or savants will never speak vain words 199; their words will be pregnant with sense. Every man had better talk sense and utter words bearing good fruit 200. It is proverbial that those who talk too much think too little or never think at all.

All scriptures condemn *adultery* or coveting another's wife or devising evil things with the pride of a confiding friend. The Christian decalogue contains a commandment against the commission of this heinous sin. Adultery is unchastity in word, thought or deed, or guilty love or uncleanness with a married person. One who commits adultery is a fool, rather a fool of fools, and is a living dead man, not reflecting a whit on his guilty action, nay, treating it as a mere trifle 141-5. Adultery breeds sin, hatred, fear and foul disgrace 146. Whatever a man's learning, wealth, status or high office, this sin makes a gnat of the mountainous man. He is a man of virtue or worth or propriety who does not look at another's dear with the eye of lust or touch her with a carnal desire 147-9. Though a man may pass virtue's bounds and do evil deeds, he is not so much condemnable or abominable as he who covets another's wife 150.

Our poet who damns an adulterer seems to be silent on the adulteress, though the treachery of the latter to plighted faith deserves severe reproof. Here are the words of a royal repentant or remorseful adulteress :—

"The shadow of another cleaves to me
And makes me one pollution.........Shall I kill myself?
What help in that? I cannot kill my sin,
If soul be soul; nor can I kill my shame;—
No, nor by living can I kill it down,
The days will grow to weeks and weeks to months,
The months will add themselves and make the years,
The years will roll into the centuries,
And mine will ever be a name of scorn."

We close this study with what Shakespeare and other great English writers have said of virtue and vice by way of caution against hasty decision in such cases.

"Virtue itself turns vice being misapplied,
And vice sometimes by action dignified".
"Virtue alone is happiness below."

"Virtue is its own reward."
"Vice is a monster of so frightful mien
As, to be hated needs to be seen;
Yet seen too oft, familiar with her face,
We first endure, then pity, then embrace."

"Vice itself lcst half its evil by losing all its grossness."

STUDY VII.

CHARACTER AND CONDUCT.

(CHAPTERS 40, 43, 46, 84-5, 90.)

Character is the resultant of soul-heritage in its transmigration acted on by culture. Literally, it is the writing of culture on the blank slate of the mind (tabula rasa) while conduct is the outward manifestation of the cultured soul or the thoroughly cultivated will, or its graceful and refined behaviour shown by outward marks of cruelty in the ordeal of society. It is a proverb that 'A tree is known by its fruits and a man is known by his actions.' Conduct is life honourable and respectable. The poet says that manners are the fruits of a loyal nature and a noble mind. Manners are said to make man; his evil manners will live in brass while his good are writ in water. Self-reliance, self-sacrifice, obedience, moral courage, or true heroism, high ideal, perseverance, moderation in views and aims, punctuality, method, and thoroughness are the distinguishing marks of good character, while good conduct is testified by love of nature, by prayer, by economy, by temperance, by life-object, and by good manners. Polonius's advice is worthy of note :

" Be thou familiar, but by no means vulgar,
Give every man thine ear but few thy voice,
Take each man's censure, but reserve thy judgement.
Costly thy habit as thy purse can buy.
Neither a borrower nor a lender be.
This, above all, to thine own self be true."

Thackeray asks what is it to be a gentleman ? Is it to be honest, to be gentle, to be generous, to be brave, to be wise and possessing all these qualities to exercise them in the most graceful outward manner". Boardman has said "Sow an act, and you reap a habit; sow a habit, and you reap a character; sow a character and you reap a destiny.' As conduct is life, character is destiny.

Culture comes of the study of books, of Nature and of Life. The eye and the ear are its avenues. Learn thoroughly what is worth learning and live worthy of your learning 391. Numbers and letters are man's two eyes 392. So the unlearned have no eyes but sores 393. The learned diffuse joy all round and make the world long for the time to meet again 394. The learned take the first while the unlearned the last rank 395. To the learned every country and town is his own 397. The pleasure of learning endures seven births 398. The more a man learns the wiser he grows 396. Learning gives pleasure to the learner as it pleases others 399. Learning is imperishable wealth and real joy 400.

Ignorance has no place in the councils of the wise. Its intrusion therein is compared to the chess play without squares 401. Its desire to shine in councils is likened to the desire of a woman without breasts for womanhood, *i.e.*, to the hoyden doating on her undeveloped charms 402. Its silence in councils will bespeak excellence 403. Its conceit will vanish as it breaks silence in the wise men's conclave 405. Its sense will pass for nonsense in the councils of wisdom 404. Ignorance is sterility, and its only value is that it exists 406. Its beauty and goodness in the absence of learning's lore are like those of the polished porcelain 407. High-born ignorance is lower in status than the low-born learning 409. Its wealth will be more fruitful of sorrow than the poverty of the learned. It is beastly by the side of choice learning as beasts compared with men 410.

Hearing is better than studying: it is wealth of wealth 411. When there is no food for the ear, let the stomach have a taste of it 412. Those well-up in the maxims of the wise enjoy heavenly delights 413. Though not born to study, listening to the wise men's words will do good in times of distress 414, for the words of the wise or good are like a staff in a slippery place 415. Those possessing the riches of the eye and the ear 'Katral-ketal udaiyar periyar' will never speak foolishly 417. It is better to listen to good, however small or slight it be 416. The unlearned ear is deaf though it hears 418. The ear devoid of lessons preached will rarely lead to modesty in speech 419. Connoisseurs by the mouth, and not by the ear may live or die without difference to the world 420.

Knowledge, derived through the eye and the ear, wards off woes and defies foes 421. Knowledge restrains wandering thoughts and turns them from evil to good 422. Though diverse sages say diversely, truth must be discerned in them all 423. Knowledge speaks acceptable good and takes in the good sense of subtle minds 424. Knowledge has no caprice, without folding or unfolding like the flower-petals 425. Knowledge knows how to live in harmony with the world wisely and well 426. Knowledge is discerning and prophetic unlike the ignorant 427. Knowledge knows what to fear and what to reject unlike the foolish 428. Knowledge foresees coming evils and averts them and so never suffers calamity 429. Knowledge is all in all and the lack of it is nothing out of nothing 430.

Character detests the base while no-character hugs them as friends 451. Character is tested by association 453 as water's taste differs with the soil over which it flows 452. Good companionship largely determines the purity of mind and purity of actions 454-5. The pure-minded will have posterity and will never do deeds that are not good 456. Good society not only earns good name as good mind earns wealth 457 ; it fortifies good mind 458. Good society or companionship is great help as wicked association is great woe 460.

Folly or *light-minded conduct* lets the gain go by and hugs loss 830. It is a defect of human nature. There is no foolery greater than doing forbidden things 831. The qualities of foolery are shamelessness (impudence), callousness to good things, harshness and aversion for every desirable thing 833. The height of folly is not to act by what is learnt, understood, and taught 834. A fool merits hell through sevenfold births 835. A fool's large fortune will make him rave like a drunken man, it will be enjoyed by his foes while his kindred starve 837. Any work attempted by the fool not only fails but fetters him with chains 836. To part company with fools will not only be pleasant but painless 839. A fool's intrusion into wise men's council will be as repugnant or repulsive as getting on the couch with unwashed feet 840.

Pretence to knowledge (pullarivu-anmai) proclaims the sorest want of knowledge while other wants the world passes over as things of inconsequence 841. A fool's cheerful gift is the outcome of the receiver's merit in a former birth : it redounds no credit to the giver 842. A fool afflicts himself with sufferings worse than what his foes can inflict on him 843. It is stupidity that arrogantly claims the glory of the wise 844. Pretence to knowledge leads men to doubt even real knowledge 845. To make a display of one's foolery is worse than exposing one's nudity 846. He who lets the mystic teachings die from his soul makes him miserable 847. The body of the fool who does not care to know his duties and neglects them when advised about them is a burden to the earth till the soul leaves it 848. One who teaches a fool who is wise in his own conceit is a fool himself 849. He who proclaims as false what the world affirms or believes in will be called a demon on earth 850.

It is *evil conduct* that disregards or offends the great, possessing rare powers 891 ; that behaves towards them without respect 892 ; that disobeys and offends law to the ruin of the offender 893 ; that does evil to the strong, beckoning Yama 894 ; that incurs the wrath of the potent 895- or of the righteous great 897 ; that disrespects hill-like or great devotees at the risk of life 896 or of eradication or of entire ruin though Indra be the delinquent 899, and that exposes one's self to the fiery anger of the great of boundless penance 900.

Every one should aim at *perfection* in character and conduct as in everything else. 'Character alone is the one which can truly save us'. 'Every one who chooses may lead a noble life.' It is more important to do right than to know it. 'Golden deeds make golden days.'

Mr. W. H. D. Adams opens his chapter on Conduct with these wise words with which we close this study: "The world judges us by our conduct ; it has neither the time nor the inclination to study our character ; moreover, it assumes that our conduct is necessarily the reflex of our character. Now it by no means follows that a man's actions are always a fair or certain indication of his judgment, his passions, or his opinions ; frequently they exaggerate or belie them, but we cannot stop to appeal from Philip drunk to Philip sober. We take him as he is and determine what he is from what he does."

STUDY VIII.

PRUDENCE AND PROSPERITY.

(CHAPTERS 47—52.)

Prudence is wisdom applied to practice or sagacity in applying means to ends. As virtuous actions are life's aims, a due consideration of the ways and means of accomplishing the ends in view becomes necessary. The work of life is judged by its moral value, and success in life depends on the doing of a right thing at the right time, at the right place, by a right person, in a right manner. In this view prudence is providence, foresight, wise economy which makes for progress or advancement, or *prosperity*.

Before proceeding to act, let every one weigh expenditure, return and profit 461, and think over it himself with his chosen friends 462. It is rashness to risk everything and lose all, tempted by cupidity 463, to undertake a thing when the issue is not clear 464 and without forming mature plans 465. It is ruinous to do an unfitting thing or to leave a fit thing undone 466. All ventures must be made after mature consideration; else they will bring disgrace 467. In the doing of a thing method is more than multitudinous help 468. However good an action may be, it is determined by the habitudes or dispositions of men for whom it is done 469. The world's esteem or approval must be the aim of every doer of good work 470.

One's own *power*, the power of the rival, the power of the support must be duly weighed with the power required for doing a thing 471. One's own ability and resources must be fully considered before beginning a venture 472. Many have suffered reverses for want of such consideration in time 473. He who breaks public peace imagining his greatness and ignoring his resources is sure to perish 474. Too much of even trifles will lead to wreckage as the axle of a wain snaps when overloaded with light peacock feathers 475. A daring climber beyond the tree's top forfeits his life 476. It is wisdom to cut one's coat according to one's cloth 477, but is folly and ruin to be spendthrifty or when expenditure much exceeds income 478. Prosperity will bid adieu to him who is too liberal or prodigal to know its extent 479-80. The sorrow's crown of sorrow is remembering the days of prosperity. Make hay while the sun shines. Time and tide waits for no man. So the *opportunity* must not be lost, and its due recognition is an act of prudence. Shakespeare has in The Tempest:—

> " There is a tide in the affairs of men
> Which, taken at the flood, leads on to fortune ;
> Omitted, all the voyage of their life
> Is bound in shallows and in miseries."

In broad daylight a crow will conquer an owl 481, and a heron waits to snap its prey 490. The right *season* binds fortune 482. Nothing is hard if done in the fit time and with proper means 483. The world may be won if attempted in season and in the proper place, or after waiting patiently for the fit season with an equable mind 485. Men who calmly wait for the opportunity are like recoiling rams 486, and, when it arrives, they do the hardest deed and promptly. A patient waiter for the fateful hour overwhelms his foe 488. Men bent upon glory will bide their time to let their hidden fires glow 487.

Next to knowing the season comes the recognition of the *place* before attacking or despising your enemy 491. Great will be the gain if skill and courage combine 492.

Weak men may prevail against the strong if they secure strong places to defend themselves 493. Hopeful victors gain without gaining coigns of vantage 494. The crocodile is strong in deep water, but it is nothing when out of the element 495. The mighty car and seaboat cannot ply in water and on land respectively 496. Fearless might will win in the right place if properly equipped 497. A leader of hosts fails in his effort to overcome an enemy, safe in his own retreat, though defended by a small band 498, or safe in his homestead though undefended and unprovisioned 499. In a slippery fen the jackal easily slays the mighty elephant with fiery eyes and tusks 500.

Place *confidence* in man after testing his virtue, cupidity, libidiousness, and fear of hazarding life 501, and in him of noble descent wearing the white flower of a blameless life 501, and of generous pride 502. Even the highly learned and the most flawless have small specks of ignorance lurking in them 503. Form an estimate of the man after scanning his good and evil qualities and seeing which preponderate 504. His deeds are the touchstone of his merit and demerit 505. Beware of confiding in kithless or kinless men who will be prone and ready to commit any crimes 506. It is the height of folly to rely on ignoramuses through partiality 507. An untried stranger should not be a confidante, for such a choice will be woeful for generations. A confidante must be chosen after long trial and, after the choice has been made, confidence must be placed in his proved prudence 509. To doubt such a chosen man will inflict unhealing wounds or cause irremediable sorrow 510.

It is prudential to secure a person of virtuous mood 511, of talent and tact who can enlarge the resources, increase wealth and avert accidents 512, and one of love, wisdom, clarified mind, and ungreediness 513. Even a choice man alters in new positions of pomp and circumstance 514. Wisdom and patient endurance unbiassed by personal attachment bespeak prudence 515. A man of prudence will duly weigh the doer, the deed and the season for doing it 516, and then entrust the duty to him 517, who has the aptitude for it 518. Prudence will never doubt or suspect an honest and steady discharger of duties, and prosperity will quit him who so doubts or suspects 519. The world prospers according as the entrusted and the tried do the right by day and by night 520.

Prudence or common sense which has the potentiality of good in it is the one thing needful for success in life : it may be called the virtue of the statesman and the legislator and the ruler. High learning and high virtue often fare ill without this commonplace commodity. Prudence is never proud but ever polite, urbane, chivalrous, and obedient ; it accommodates itself to circumstance ; a reasonable and prudent submission achieves its one sole aim which is worldly success and prosperity.

STUDY IX.

HEALTH AND WEALTH.

(CHAPTERS 95, 101.)

Health is not merely diseaselessness or painlessness but more. Health of body and health of mind are the two divisions of the subject. The human body is a standing miracle. It is constituted like the glorious rainbow. 'There is but one temple in the Universe' says Novalis, 'and that is the body of man'. *Mens sana in corpore sano, i.e.*, a sound mind in a sound body, shows the intimate relationship between the two. " The *mens sana* which in conjunction with the *corpore sana* we rightly put forward as the chief pledge and earnest to earthly happiness, must also be *mens pura* unprofaned by indulgence of irregular and illicit desires." The sanitary conditions of health are pure air, pure water, sound and timely sleep, wholesome food, clean clothing, good climate, high and dry habitation, and congenial work. "Our ancestors" writes Sir John Lubblock "lived more in the country, more in the open air, more in agricultural operations. We are to a much greater extent concentrated in cities, work much more in houses, shops and factories; our occupations are sedentary and stooping and are a greater tax on the brain and nervous system." While our vitality is affected by insanitation, by excitement, by fret and worry, cheerfulness, good humour and peace of mind promote it. When we are out of sorts, things get on our nerves, the most trifling annoyances assume the proportions of a catastrophe."

Health is conducive to work, physical and mental, and work is wealth, and therefore *health is wealth.* Wealth is acquired by right means or wrong, enjoyed well or ill, and spent in good or evil ways, in beneficence or maleficence. The right means of acquiring wealth are agriculture in the first place, and trade and commerce next, and the wrong means are force and fraud. To embrace the former and eschew the latter knits individuals into societies and keeps them up and cements them and brings about solidarity amongst them.

Hindus treat of *food* as medicine, and all the culinary preparations are so many health-giving medicines. Diseases arise from mistakes in diet and other things. An excess or deficiency of wind, bile or phlegm, say the learned medicos, causes disease 941. There will be no disease and no necessity for medicine in case of good digestion 942. Food may be eaten after thorough digestion and in moderation 943 to lengthen life. It is good to eat moderately what is agreeable when hungry 944 without risk to life 945. Gluttony breeds diseases 945. A gormandizer knows neither the measure of fire in his stomach nor any laws of health and begets swarms of diseases 947. In such cases the physician should first diagnose the disease, find out its nature and cause, and then determine the best treatment and method of cure by consulting the best medical writers 948. Before undertaking treatment, he must take into consideration the patient's condition or state of health at the time and the season of the year, in addition to the ascertainment of the nature of the disease 949. Medical science consists of four parts and speaks of four things—the patient, the physician, the medicine and the attendant or compounder.

The poet emphasises good digestion, moderate eating, and good appetite as prophylactics, and lays stress on careful diagnosis, faithful treatment, proper medicine and expert medical knowledge as the requisites of a doctor.

We have already adverted to wealth in the hands of the noble-hearted 216-7, of kindliness 246, as unstable 332, as glorious 363, as happiness, to the wealth of books 375, 400, of the ear 411, of the niggardly 437, of fools 837, of the ancestral 937, and of the churl 1000. Here we speak of wealth without benefaction. The possessor of such wealth is reckoned as dead 1001, as a demon 1002, and as a burden to the earth 1003, and the miser thus hated here will have nothing as his own in the other world 1004. The miser who neither gives nor enjoys is really poor 1005 and he who relieves not the wants of the worthy is a churl 1006, and he who gives nothing to the destitute is like a beautiful old maiden who lives in single blessedness 1007. The miser is an *etty* (poisonous) tree amidst a populous town 1008, and his hoard of wealth will be inherited by strangers 1009. The brief poverty of the generous man of wealth is like the temporary dryness of a rainy cloud 1010.

Ben Jonson's advice ' to get money, still get money, no matter by what means ' is unwholesome. Wealth is said to be dirt in the right place. John Heywood says:

" *The loss of wealth is loss of dirt,*
As sages in all times assert ;
The happy man's without a shirt "

and Goldsmith gives the dictum " that ill fares the land to hastening ills a prey where wealth accumulates and men decay" and describes the peasant's innocence and health as his best companions, and the ignorance of wealth as his best riches. This is only a half-truth, but half-truths are pernicious in their effects and are somtimes worse than falsehoods. Wealth commands labour, leisure, credit, and comfort, if one knows how to use it aright, but it entails drudgery and anxiety and misery when wealth possesses a man instead of man possessing wealth. Good and regular habits as 'early to bed and early to rise' make a man healthy, wealthy and wise.

Locke writes: "What concerns the body and health reduces itself to these few and easily observable rules: plenty of *open air*, *exercise and sleep*, *plain diet*, *no wine or strong drink* and very little or *no physick*, not too warm and strait *clothing*, especially the *head* and *feet* kept cold, and the feet often used to cold water and exposed to wet."

Bacon, who says that riches are "the baggage of virtue", advises thus: "Seek not proud riches, but such as thou mayst get justly, use soberly, distribute cheerfully and leave contentedly. Yet have no abstract nor friarly contempt of them. The improvement of the ground is the most natural obtaining of riches; for it is our great mother's blessing, the earth's; but it is slow. And yet where men of great wealth do stoop to husbandry, it multiplieth riches exceedingly".

"The two great dangers of health" say Storr and Gibson, "are a tendency to lose sight of humanitarian in economical principles and money worship".

STUDY X.

KING AND STATE.

(CHAPTERS 39, 44-6, 54-57, 59, 64-78, 86-9, AND 24).

Some of the chapters under " Arasial " apply to men in general and have, therefore, been handled in the three preceding Studies. In this Study the chapters bearing on Royalty proper are taken up for consideration. The king is but a man and, like every other man, is expected to possess the wealth of books and of oral instruction, to be wise and to act on mature consideration of time, place, circumstance, resources, succour, etc. 'Kings are like stars—they rise and set, they have the worship of the world but no repose.' 'Divinity hedges a king.' 'The king's name is a tower of strength.' 'Kings are tyrants from policy when subjects are rebels on principle.' These quotations indicate the dignity, duties and responsibilities of kings. " Uneasy lies the head that wears the crown." This verse expresses the incessant watchfulness and cares and anxieties of royalty.

The terms used to denote the king are 'arasan' 'vendhan' 'lord of land' 'mannan' and 'mannavan' and a great king, according to our poet, owns six things—army, people, wealth, minister, friends, and fort, and four qualities—courage, liberality, wisdom, and energy. He should be prompt and decisive, virtuous and graceful 381-4. He should collect the revenue, keep the coffer full, defend his kingdom, and expend from the state treasury what may be needed for its welfare 385. He should be easily accessible and speak no harsh or unpleasant word. Such a king's praise is on the lips of the world and he commands its obedience 385-7. He who guards the realm and maintains strict justice is deified by his subjects 388. If he gives his ear to bitter counsels, he is a worthy king whose power keeps the world in peace and safety 389. What glorify a king are gifts, right sceptre, grace, and care of people's weal 390.

The first and most important duty of a king is to *correct himself.* He should check arrogance, put down wrath, and restrain his meanness 431. He should curb niggardliness, pride and unseemly mirth lest disgrace come upon him 432. A small fault in a king will loom large in the eye of the world and, as fault, will prove fatal. A king should be free from faults 434. He should anticipate the evil times, else his joy will consume away like straw before the fire 435. He should scan and remove his own faults before he does those of others 436. He should not be miserly and leave undone what should be done 437, for avarice is the worst of faults 438. He should never indulge in self-complaisant moods or in vain desires 439. Evil counsels will prove harmless if a king cherishes his love unknown to his foes 440.

A king should have about him *men of virtue, wisdom* and *worth* and all accomplishments, whose counsel will remove the present ills and avert the future ones 441-2. Men of mighty souls must be cherished and appropriated as precious and rare treasure 443 ; such cherished friends are a tower of strength to monarchs 444. As counsellors are a monarch's eyes, they should be selected with wise counsel 445. The friendship of worthy men is a bulwark to a king 446. Faithful ministers who will boldly reproach the erring king will be a strong defence to him 447, and the want of such men by the king's side will bring about his ruin 448. Kings without true friends will know no stability, as he who owns no capital can have no gain of interest 449. If kings forego worthy friends, their foes will multiply and their woes will be tenfold 450.

Wise kings will eschew *mean associates* 451. The wisdom of kings will be tested by their companions as the quality of water by the soil through which it flows 452. Self-forgetfulness in excess of joy will forfeit glory, praise, and blessing, and will bring about repentance 431-5. Therefore kings should be watchful, energetic and thoughtful to achieve glories 536-8. At moments of great exultation kings had better ponder over the fall of scornful minds 539. Good remembrance obtains the wished-for gain 540.

A *good king* will be just and impartial, take advice and act 541. He will be held dear as rain drops 442. He will promote learning and sagely virtue 543. He will win the hearts of the subjects who will embrace his feet 544. The land of a king who rules by just laws will be blessed with showers and will have abundance 545. Equitable rule, not lance, gains victory for the king 546. If the king guards his realm, justice guards him 547. The king who hears no grievances and, hearing, does not examine evidence and pass judgment, will go to ruin 548. To punish the wicked with death will be to weed out the field of corn 550.

He is a *cruel* king and a worse murderer who is unjust and harasses his subjects 551, who extorts gifts from them 552, who makes no daily search for wrongs or who rules unjustly 553, who swerves from right and refuses counsel 554, and who makes his subjects weep bitterly 555. Tyranny loses people, wealth, realm and glory 556. The absence of kingly grace is like the drought to thirsty souls 557. To be subject to tyranny is more painful than poverty 558. The land of a tyrant who makes unrighteous gain will have no proper seasons nor rain from heaven 559. In a tyrant's country cows will yield less milk and sages forget their sacred lore 560.

A *good* king duly investigates and punishes crimes with a view to deter them 561, and raises the rod with severe brow but lets it fall gently 562, but he is an unjust king who lets wrongs go unpunished 563. As *vox populi* is *vox dei*, the subjects' wail over a king's cruelty will hasten his death and extinguish his joys 564. Terrorism (harsh words and severe punishments) in a king deprives him of his wealth 565, of his life 566, and of his conquering pride 567. A *negligent* king who reproves in wrathful mood will lose his prosperity 568. A king who neglects to build a fort whence to defy his foe will suffer death in time of war 569. Tyrants taking fool's counsels will prove a heavy burden to the mother Earth 570.

In primitive times *force* ruled the country ; the civil king was also the military leader. When civilisation commenced, *council* had its place. The king consulted councillors as an advisory body. The fable of Jupiter marrying Metis and eating her up when pregnant and delivering Minerva (Pallas) in perfection out of his head illustrates the statement. A good king takes advice but issues his edict independently and on mature consideration and in his own person. With the growth of cities and of multiplied interests, the government came to be vested practically in the *cabinet* or in the *privy council*, and the maxim " A king can do no wrong " absolved the king of his direct responsibility and answerability. The ministry became mainly responsible for good government.

A minister must be a man of tact and skill in the choice of means, time and mode for executing any undertaking 631, and should possess firmness, cleverness perseverance and zeal for protecting the people's well-being 632. His tact will be manifest in effecting discords amongst enemies, in maintaining the goodwill of friends and in recalling seceders 633. His duty lies in a complete comprehension of a matter, in executing it in the best manner possible and in offering advice of assurance in crisis 634. The best minister is one well-posted in all matters 635 and one who combines in himself acuteness and learning 636 and understands the ways of the world and acts accordingly 637. It is the minister's concern to educate even an ignorant king with sound advice 638. If he means ill to his master, he is more dangerous than hosts (seventy crores) of enemies 639. A project well-planned will fail, should the ministry lack executive ability 640.

The ministry should possess eloquence and guard itself against careless speech 641-2 as loss and gain depend upon it. The speech must be such as to inspire desire in those who have not heard it 643. It must be adapted to the audience 644 and not such as can be refuted 645. It should be charming to the hearer and bring out the sense of the speeches of others 646. A man, mighty in word, possessing good memory and of fearless speech, cannot be over-reached by any hostile power 647. When powerful oratory propounds a weighty theme, the world will be all ear to him 648. A man not accustomed to brevity will be profuse in his speech 649, and one who cannot expound his learning to others in a convincing manner will be like a scentless flower bound in a blooming garland 650.

A minister must be pure in his action and do only what will bring glory and good to his king 651-2. He must shun the rest 653. He may err, but his error should not recur; his outlook must be on permanency 654. If he does so, he need not repent 655. His mother may be hungry, but his action must be uninfluenced by her hunger 656. Poverty is gain; reproof will ward off anguish; good deeds will always be blessed; no wrong can protect a state 657-60.

Power in action is the outcome of power of mind. Hence obstacles should be overcome by pressing onward and success achieved. It is easy to advise but hard to carry out the advice. A king will accept the actions of great men who are steadfast in their will. Dwarfs men may be in form, but giants they will be in action. They are often the linch-pin of the mighty car of state. The right thing should be done at all hazards if pleasure should be won at last. He who desires power in action is the crown of all the rest 661-70.

Resolve is counsel's end. Don't sleep when action is imperative. Be prompt and watchful. Trifles neglected will cause ruin. Money, means, time, place, action, success, obstacles should be duly weighed. Consult the proficient and the experienced. Go step by step. Make foes friends. When petty princes tremble, their subjects submit to mightier kings 671-80.

Though the substance of some of these chapters has been absorbed in the consideration of virtues and vices, it is reproduced here as they are applicable more to ministers and their actions. It is a merry definition of Sir Henry Wotton that "An ambassador is an *honest* man sent to *lie* abroad for the commonwealth." The honest man of an ambassador is resident in a foreign country as a king's agent to protect the interests of his mother country and is often obliged to tell lies or falsehoods on his country's behalf.

Benevolence, high birth, courtesy, love, knowledge, choice, powerful and pleasant words, learning, sense, goodly grace, conciseness, fearlessness in emergency, home-thrust, integrity, resolution and resourcefulness are the attributes of an *envoy* who goes on his king's errand. He consults time, place, and ponders before he delivers his embassy or speaks his mandate. An envoy recks not death to himself who means advantage to his lord 681-90.

A king's *counsellor* should be neither too far nor too near his king, as a man desiring warmth neither approaches the hearth fire nor keeps himself afar. A minister should not be covetous nor commit serious blunders lest he rouse his lord's suspicion. In the presence of the sovereign he should neither whisper to nor smile at others. He should not be a Paul Pry but wait for divulgement of royal secrets. In case he has to make suggestions to his king, he should do what is desirable in a pleasing manner. His advice must be agreeable. He should not think lightly or behave unbecomingly for the reason that the king is junior to him in age, or is his kinsman or that he enjoys the royal esteem or is too familiar with him 691-700.

A *minister* who is able to read the king's mind like a God will be of great worth to a king. Such *thought-reading* ministers may be one in shape and form with others, but differ in the calibre of their minds. Among the means of thought-reading the *face* and the *eyes* stand foremost. The face is an index of the mind and it is bright or gloomy in consonance with the joy or gloom of the mind. If a king has thought-readers by his side, he should simply stand looking at their face. The thought-reading ministers can easily discover the lurking hatred or love of foreign rulers.

The measuring rod of ministerial acuteness will be found to be their own eyes and naught else 701-710.

Words must be studied as regards their order, their uses or their character, and speakers in council must be masters of words. They must ascertain the nature of the assembly and consult the suitable time. Ministers should be lights in the assembly of the wise and should profess crass ignorance in that of fools. Modesty will be a virtue in a council of superiors, and a blundering minister in such a council will be like a virtuous man falling away from his path. The learned will shine in the council of the learned, who can scan the values of words. It is superfluous and useless to lecture to the wise. Impressive speakers in wise councils will keep mum in an unwise assembly; if they speak, their words will be like nectar spilt in the sewer or will be like pearls cast before the swine.

A minister should *not dread* the council. He who knows the forces of words can discern the moods of the council and does never fail in his discourse 721; he who is master of the incisiveness of words will be conspicuous in the wise men's assembly. Fearlessness in a public speaker will hold its ground. Clever speakers imitate the speech-virtue of men more learned than they. The study of dialectics will help to make an apt reply in councils. He who knows science and dreads the council is as useless as the sword in a coward's hand or in that of a hermaphrodite. Such a man is worse than an illiterate and is as good as dead 722-30.

The essentials of a *State* are *land*, *fort*, *army*, *military spirit* and *wealth*. A good country is ever fertile, has virtuous and wealthy men; it yields abundance and knows no calamity; it pays tributes to the king even when other burdens press it; it is free from famine, plague and other ravages; from factions, internecine strife and lawless men. The best country is ever peaceful and fruitful without labour and despite invasions; is well-watered by rains and springs, has a mountain near feeding its rivers and owns a stronghold. To sum up, unfailing health, fertility, joy, sure defence, and wealth are its jewels. All these jewels will lose their sheen when the land is not at peace with its king 731-40 or rises in revolt against him.

A *fortress* is wealth to aggressors and defenders alike. Its essentials are a never-failing fount, an open space, a hill, and a shady forest near. It must be high, broad, strong, and inaccessible according to the science of fortification. It must be able to defy all the energy of the foe, be impregnable to assailants and javelins, have a good commissariat for defence; it must have ample munitions and such reserves to be used in times of need as to give victory to its defenders; it should dismay strong foes at the outset and gain greatness in battle day after day. To the craven, no fortress is strong enough 741-50.

The *sources* of the *royal revenue* are inherited wealth, kist, booty, tribute, excise, customs and finds or treasure-troves. Without wealth the insolence of foes cannot be checked or put down 756, 759.

More important than the sinews of war, is a *conquering host*, well-equipped and dauntless 761, and a veteran host, ever brave. The breath of the dragon drives away the squeaking angry mice. That is a *veteran* host which has suffered no defeats or desertions but is famed for its old hereditary courage. That is a *conquering* host which joins its ranks and withstands sudden and deadly onsets. That is a *warlike* host that shows valour with honour and makes sure advance in the path of glory and is confident of its success.

A valiant army that is well disciplined and marshalled and goes on to brave the enemy despite onslaught, or that is well equipped and drilled, will gain applause though not skilled in war either offensive or defensive. Victory is sure if the army is neither weak, poor, nor cowardly. Hosts of soldiers thirsting for war do not make an army if they have no commanders or *generals* to lead them, 761-70.

As "a jewel in a ten-times barred-up chest is a bold spirit in a loyal breast", a host without the *military spirit* is no army. Every fighter should challenge his foe and glory in the *Vira-Kal* or stone of heroism. The foe should be no timid hare but an elephant to earn praise. In the field of battle he should be fierce as tiger but kind to the vanquished. A warrior hurls the dart in hand and plucks the javelin with a cheerful heart from his wounded breast. A fearless warrior will never wink his eye at the sight of the flight of the enemy's javelin. A sterling warrior counts that day lost when he sustains no glorious wound. A fame-loving warrior will be regardless of his life, ever girding up his loins or wearing ankle rings as a sign of his heroism. He rushes wherever the tide of battle rolls, not caring for or undamped by the sovereign's reproof. A true hero, though vanquished, will die to keep up his vow. Glorious death is a desirable boon to a hero for whom the sovereign's eyes overflow with tears 771-80.

Hostility breeds disunion and is a grievous plague to shun. It ceases when malice dies and, when it ceases altogether, victory is certain. Men who, out of enmity, work woes will never be great, or those who cherish enmity for enmity's sake are grievously faulty and embrace death. A soul mastered by enmity reaps rain. Enmity is cherished by men of misfortune and not by men of fortune. Enmity is the fountain head of all evils, as friendship is that of all good.

It is folly to court the fray with *a strong foe*, when he has neither the love of kinsmen nor the strength of friends 861-2. A craven is he who knows nothing, agrees with none, gives away nothing and falls an easy prey to his foeman; whose wrath blazes at the disclosure of every secret; who scans no right path, whom no precepts bind and no crimes affright, and who owns no grace of good; who is blind in his race and whose lustful passions swell. Such an one is liked by and is the delight of his foeman. His deeds will be unseemly and any one who proffers aid to him is sure to buy his hate. The foe rejoices, for none will claim kindred with the man of many faults and no graces. If the foes are ignorant and timid, woe to them, but all hail victory to their antagonists. The craven, the illiterate, and the angry, will never win glory 862-70.

Shun *hate* from your bosom; the hate of word-ploughers more than that of the bow-ploughers. He is a forlorn wretch who is scorned by all. The world holds him dear who turns foes to friends. When there are two foes, it is wisdom to make one your devout friend. Distress quells questions of difference or agreement. It is folly to disclose your infirmities to your enemies. The means of putting an end to the proud hate of your foe are knowledge of them, doing one's part aright, and self-defence. Nip it in the bud, for the thorn growing hard will prick and wound the hand that plucks it. In case the pride of haters is not quelled, the foe will not let you even breathe 871-80.

Inward enmity is infinitely worse than open hate. Treachery in friendship is baneful. Open hostility, with daggers drawn, is not to be dreaded as enmity in friendship's guise.

Lurking hate will cut a deeper wound in troublous times. Secret enmities pervert minds and suffer deadly affliction from unkind kinsmen and destruction and breed disunion in a house where harmony should prevail, as between a casket and its cover. Concealed hate, as the file does the gold, wastes away the strength of a house. Hidden enmity, though small as a shred of sesame seed, will work ruin in the end. To live in a house with those who don't agree is to keep company with a snake in a shed or hut.

The influence of the *harem* on majestic sovereigns as on the generality of mankind is always nefarious and destructive; but there are exceptions, where the queens are good, pious souls dreading sins and sinful acts. What our poet deprecates here is being led by women or obeying their behests, in other words, the loss of self-respect by men who lose their wits, love-laden or passion-ridden. As courtesans or prostitutes pretend love and affection only for the sake of money, their mal-influence need not be doubted. Yet in all Tamil epics of fancy, worth or merit, chapters are devoted to Royal visits to haunts of whoredom and passing nights in the harlot's dear embrace. As the devil finds scripture-texts in defence of its devilry, the brothel-haunters never lack reasons, rather readily hit upon the rationale for the continuance of the demon-like institution on the score of convenience and home-relief.

What all good souls seek is *fame*, and what ill-souls incur is *infamy*. One is as enduring as the other. Ascetics are callous to either and have their eye on the cessation of birth. But true ascetics are drops in the ocean of humanity. Fame is the goal of householders and rulers of realms alike. It is a spur to noble minds, irrespective of birth and status, to scorn delights and live laborious days, though it does not grow on mortal soil. As too much praise or arch-flattery is scandal in disguise, every good man may be ambitious of modest fame as he knows that it will, like a river, bear away things light and swollen, the straws and froth, and preserve in its bed the solid gold.

" Good name in man and woman, dear my lord,
Is the immediate jewel of their souls.
Who steals my purse, steals trash ; it is something, nothing ;
'T was mine, 't is his, and has been a slave to thousands ;
But he that filches from me *my good name*,
Robs me of that which not enriches him,
And makes me poor indeed ".

" The purest treasure mortal times afford
Is *spotless reputation* ; that away,
Men are but gilded loam or painted clay"—
Shakespeare.

A good name is, therefore, more precious than wealth or riches and better than a precious ointment, as the scripture has it. Bacon says that fame or praise, or glory is the reflection of virtue, and our poet says,

" Fame is virtue's child, they say ; if, then,
You childless live, you live the scorn of men". 238.

STUDY XI.

THE INFLUENCE OF KURAL.

The *Garland of Tiruvalluv* is made up of appreciations of the poet and analyses of his masterpiece, the Sacred Kural, by the master-minds of old. The words and thoughts of the noble and illustrious poem have been freely indented on by his successors of the poetic fraternity both with and without acknowledgments.

That the poet's contemporary, Seetthalai Satthanar, of the second century, an acute literary critic, has quoted a couplet (55) in his *Manimekalai* or 'The Gem-Belt' xxii, 59—61 and characterised the author as a Poet of Truth.

> " Theivam tho!a! Ko!unat-to!uthe!uval
> Peyyena peyyum peruma!ai yenna,
> *Poyyil pulavan* poru!urai therāy."

' She (the wife) will adore no other deity than her husband whom she worships as soon as she wakes up and then rises from her bed and whose invocation for heavy rain will be immediately complied with. Know the significance of the words of the poet of naught but truth.'

Ilanko-Adigal, a Chera prince and author of *Silappathikaram*, has made a similar use of the Kural. The opening lines of the 21st canto of this Epic-drama contain, or repeat with certain transpositions, the Kural couplet 319 :

> ' Murpahal seithān piran kedu than kedu
> Pirpahal Kaankruum petri thān nar-pahalae.'

In the epic of *Chintamani* Tiru-thakka-Thevar has done likewise. *Vide* viii Iḷambakam, St. 3 and St..39.

" Thoḷutha-tham-kayyi-nullum— thiru-mudi-ahatthum sora
Aḷutha kanneeri - nullum - anikalatth - ahatthum-māynthu
Paluthü-kaṉ-irinthu-kollum-padai-yudan-odunkum."

Vide Kural 828. ' Tholutha-kai-yullum, etc '

" Idatthodu-poḷuthu-naadi-evvinaik-kannum-anjār.
Thadatthidai kakkai yontrae yayiram-kodi koohai
Idatthidai yaḷunga chentru-aangu-innuyir-sehuttha-thantrae."

Vide Kurals 481 and 500.

' Pahal vellum-kookaiyai-kaakkai,' ' Kaalaḷ-kaḷaril-nari-yadum.'

Stanzas 31 and 32 summarise the duties of a good king in the manner of Kural.

Vide, Ilambakam X, st. 19.

" Maanak-kavari maṉivan-dahatra "

is an echo of ' Mayir-neepin-vaḷa-kavari-mā ' 969.

Valaiyapathi, one of the panchakaaviyams, which is still in the land of the dead, has some echoes of Kural in the stray stanzas to hand. *Vide* chapter Thuravu 8.

" *Matrum thodarppā devenkol pirapparukka*
Luttark-kudambu mikai yavai yuḷvaḷi
Patrā vinai yay palapala yonikal
Atrā yuḷalum arutthark-karithey."

Vide Kural 345.

In *Purananuru* 34, ll. 6-7, there is a reference to the Ara-Iyal of Kural, 110, on Gratitude.

> ' Nilampudai peyarva thāyinum oruvan
> *Seythi kontrarku kuithi illena*
> *Aram pāditrae.*'

Here 'Aram pāditrae' is interpreted as the God of Virtue, or Thevar Valluvar sang, and the Kural couplet is simply paraphrased in the second line.

> " Ennantri kontrarkum yui vundaam, yui villai
> Seynantri kontra maharku".

Kamban's *Ramayanam* of the 11th c. is prolific in the use of Kural lines and sentiments, *vide* Veḷvippadalam, St. 33, in which the Emperor Mahabali chastises Sukrachari's advice.

> ' Yedutthu oruvaruk—koruvar-eevathanin-munnae
> Thaduppathu-ninak-kalakitho-thakaivil veḻḻi,
> Koduppathu vilakku kodiyoi, vunathu suttram
> Vuduppathuvum vunpathuvum intri *vidu* kintrāy.'

This contains or embodies couplet 166 'Kodupathu aḻukkaruppan sutram uduppathu-vum Unpathuvu-mintri-kedum'.

In the same padalam, st. 29, occurs the Kural sentiment expanded into a quatrain.

> " Velliyai yāthal viḻambinai, melore
> Velliya-raka vaḷankuva thallal
> Eḻḻuva yen'sila innuyir enum
> *Koḻḻutal theethu, koduppathu nantraal.*"

The Kural couplet runs as follows:

> " Nallareninum koḷal theethu, melulakam
> Illeninum eethalae nantru". 222.

The same padalam, stanza 32, condemns miserliness or 'ulopam' in strong terms thus: 'Yul-therru Vempakai yāvathu ulopam,' and the evils of this vice are put forth in st. 43 of Thadakai-vathai-padalam.

"Ulapparum piṉippura ulopa montru mae
Alapparum guṉankaḷai yaḷikku maarupole."

These verses echo Kural couplet 438, beginning 'Patrulla mennum *ivaranmai.*' Instances can be multiplied.

The *Devaram* of St. Appar of the 7th C. has numerous echoes of Kural. 'Ilaittha naalellai kadappathu', Part III Tiru-Arur Pathikam 31, echoes Kural 779 'Ilaittha thikavamai saavārai.' The couplet 202 beginning 'Theeyavai theeya payatthalaal' has its echo in Book II 97. 7 (concluding line). 'Yun kaḷaladi servilarkatku *theeyavai theeyavae.*' The hymn 64 of Part I, entitled *Thiru-veeli-milalai,* has, in stanza 3. 'Varunthina *nerunal intraai,*' which is in substance a duplicate of 'Nerunal luḷinnoruvan intillai yennum Perumai yudai thivvulaku.' 336.

Umapathi Sivam, one of the Saiva Kuravars of the 12th C. has quoted Kural 348 in his *Nenjuvidu Thoothu.*

"Thalaippattāar theera thuranthār, mayanki
Valaippattaar matraiyavar-entru-nilaithamiḷin
Theivappulamai Tiruvalluva ruraittha
Meivaittha sollai virumbamal.'

The *Thirukkhalittu-paadiyar* of Yuyya-Vantha-Theva-Nayanar has many Kural couplets embodied in stanzas. Stanzas 34 and 40 enshrine Couplets 359 and 362 respectively.

The *Nalayira Pirabandam* of the great Alwars has been influenced by the Kural couplets. St. Nammalvar of the 9th C has in I ii 5.

> " Attrathu patrenil utrathu veeduyir
> Setrathu mannuril Attirai patrae,"

which reproduces Kural 350.

In Part IV vi. 10 occurs ' Unnitthu matroru theivam thoḷaḷ-avanaiyaḷlal,' which is an obvious reproduction of the famous couplet ' Theivam thoḷal '. Vide *ante.*

> " Kandu k'ettu yutru monthu-vundu-vuḷalum aiyn-karuvi
> Kanda-vinpam-therivariyā vaḷavilla-sittinpam ".

repeats Kural 1101 in Puṉarchi-mahil-thal.

In Part V vii. 3, there is ' Poruḷallatha vennai porulākki ' which echoes Kural 751. ' Porulallavarai Porulaaha seyyum '.

In the same Part the hymn entitled 'Massaru Sothi ' contains in st. 4 the line ' Ooravar kavvai yeru vittu annai sol Neer padutthu', which is but a reproduction of Kural 1147. " Ooravar kavvai yeruvaha annai sol
Neerāha neeḷum innoi."

In ' Peria-Thiru-madal ' couplets 37-39.

> " Kamatthin
> Mannum vaḷi muraiyae nitru naamānokkil
> *Anna nadaiyar alaresa aadavar mel*
> *Mannu madaluraar yenpathore* vasakamum
> *Thennuraiyil kettariva thundn* "

echo the verse 1137 " Kadalanna Kāma mulanthum madalerā Pennir perunthakka thil."

In the quotation from the Madal the expression 'thennurai' means 'the sonthern tongue,' or 'the sweet speech,' or a periphrasis for Kural.

St. Thayumanar of the early 18th c was no exception to the rule. 'Perul-Vaṉakkam,' st. 12 makes use of the very first Kural in

" Ahara vuyir elutthu anaithumaki veraay
Amarntha then ahilānda manaitthu māhi."

His famous quotation from 'Sacchithanantha Sivam,' st. 5.

" Intraik kiruntbārai naalaik-kiruppa rentru
Eṉṉavoe thida millai yae "

is a recast or paraphrase of the Kural 'Neru nel-uḻan oruvan intrillai."

Similarly, the two verses from 'Ninai vontru,' ll. 3-4,

Guru moliae malai ilakku,
Matrai moḷi yellam
Kodintri vattadal koḻva thokkum "

are reminiscent of the Kural 401. 'Arankintri vattadi yatrae.'

'Ponnai maatharai' section, stanza 36,

" *Katrumen palan katridu noon murai*
Sotra sorhaḻ sukarambamoe neri
Nitral vendum etc."

reminds the reader of the Kural 2.

" Katrathanaa laaya paya nenkol, vaalarivan
Natrāḻ thola renin."

Among the poems of the latter part of the eighteenth century 'Somesar Muthumoli Venba' by Sivagnana Yogigal and 'Vadamalai Venba' by Ekachandagrahi, an admirer of Vadamalai Pillayan, the ruler of Tinnevelly and maker of the great "Maccha Purānam' in Tamil close each stanza with a choice Kural couplet containing apt historical or mythological illustrations. Hereunder are given two stanzas from these once schoolboy-favourites, one from each, as specimens.

" Ponmalayin vengai poritthu meendān *Senni*
Thonmai vali-yaṉmayināl somesā—Pannin
Madi ila mannavan yeithum adi yaḷanthan
Thaaya-thellām orungu." Kural 610.

The heroism of Karikal Peru Vaḷathan, the Chola King (Senni) who conquered the countries up to the Himalayas and had his tiger emblem engraved on the mountains is utilised to illustrate the results of tireless energy.

The *Muthumoli Venba* comprises 133 stanzas at the rate of one stanza for each chapter in Kural, whereas the *Vadamalai Venba* has only 108 stanzas, omitting the *Inba Iyal.* Stanza 54 on *unforgetfulness* embodies the Kural 534.

" Aaṉ maranthu nalhi adavi idai yonthiyay.
Maṉipan vanthaan Vadamalaiyae—maanilatthu
Accha mudaiyarku aran illai, aangillai
Pocchap pudaiyarku nanku."

A volume can be written on the subject of the influence of Kural, and it is hardly possible to comprise hosts of illustrations in a single study. The reader can add to those given here as he advances in his study of Tamil poetry.

Six years ago the third section of Kural, entitled Kamatthu or Inba-pāl, was reproduced in dramatic form in prose by Mr. Seeni Govindarajan, and its presentation of the twenty-five Chapters in clear analysis with choice Kural couplets by way of illustration is admirable. Every Tamil Youth can go through it with pleasure and profit.

The *Righteous* or *'Kural' Lullaby* by Pandit Isvaramurthi Pillai, published some seventeen years ago, for his daughter's children, is a favourite of the *belle monde.* It contains 133 poetic wreaths or kannis and each is fragrant with the sweet thought of a prominent couplet in each chapter. It is *virginibus puerisque.* It is taken in with the mother's milk in the child's waking moments and it gently gets in through the ear as the fond mother lulls her dozy darling. The growing child innocently babbles out the sagely maxim in its playful moments and, like Pippa, unconsciously sets right the delinquency of adult mankind.

Thus it will be clear that this great world-classic, *Kural,* has, since the day of its publication in the third Sangam, permeated almost every great work in Tamil literature either on behalf of the Jaina, Buddhistic, Saivite, Vaishnavite or other religion or intended for the promotion of human character and conduct from a moral point of view.

STUDY XII.

CLOSING STUDY.

In the Opening Study the thought of the poet and the value of his immortal poem were considered. Here in the Closing Study attention will be paid to the poet's art in the conveyance of his high ideas. The kural-venba of four and three feet, the last foot being catalectic and every other foot enjoying the license of being dissylabic or trisyllabic and bearing the accent on any syllable was almost the poet's invention for his purpose. Each couplet or distich is said to be 'an apple of gold in a network of silver' and carries the maximum of sense in a minimum of words. It is terse and concise and epigrammatic and has been compared to a semi-perforated mustard seed with the contents of the seven seas. The language of the poem is pure tamil, and its capacity to express any thought, witty, humorous and subtle, is evidenced in each couplet. There are not more than fifty Sanskrit words, it is said, in this poem of twelve thousand words. Like some other Sangam poetry, it refutes the futile argument of the monopolising Sanskritist that its vocabulary will not do for expressing subtle or recondite or scientific thoughts. It bristles with wit, humour, and gentle irony couched in expressions 'Jewels five words long that shine on the forefinger of all time,' and its verbal melody is deftly managed by the choice alternation or arrangement of vowels and consonants. Telling phrases, apt similes and comparisons, striking personifications, gentle hyperboles, and innuendoes, sparkle in every page and at every turn. The wit, humour and irony are conspicuous in the soliloquies and dialogues of the third part on love, *vide* chapters 132 entitled

'Feigned Anger or Petty Jealousies'. Hyperboles abound in chapters 112, 113, 127 on Beauty, Praise and Mutual Desire respectively. Apt similes and comparisons are numerous and odorous. They are derived from common objects and circumstances. 'Like the hairs from off the head that fall to earth' 964 illustrates the loss of status. As the hand of him whose vesture slips away' 788 sincere friendship; 'Like those that warm themselves at the fire' 691 the conduct in the presence of the king; 'Like the beauties that appear in a poem the often one reads and ponders' 783, the pleasures of friendship; 'Like the sharp file...........Like the tree' 997 the men of sharp wit .... those void of courtesy; Like ignorance detected the more the men learn' 1110, the rejoicing in the embrace; Like the moon seized by the dragon 1146 for the slanderous rumour; 'Like the full tank amidst the village' 215, the wealth of the good; Like the bird leaving its nest when fledged' 338, the relationship between body and soul; 'Like the cow in tiger's skin' 273, the inconsistent conduct; Like the scentless flower in bunches or nosegays' 650, the learned men without the power of speech; Like the Ka (vadi) 1116 for passion on both sides; 'As man's shadow dogs his steps wherever he wends', 208, ruin chasing sinful deeds; 'Like the chaste lady' 974, greatness; *vide* chapter 108 on meanness or vileness. Full comparisons are frequently met with.

> 'Water springs in sandy pits deeper they are dug,
> So, knowledge increases oftener it is learnt' 396.

Compared objects are often implied and need to be made explicit; Compare

> 'Needs not in words to dwell on virtue's fruits.
> 'The man in litter borne with them that toiling bear'
> 37.

Humour and irony seem to be combined in verses 336, 340.

> " Existing yesterday to-day to nothing hurled !
> *Such greatness owns this transitory world* "

Here the word 'greatness' is used ironically and the irony is indicated by the word 'transitory'.

> " The soul in fragile shed as lodger courts repose :
> *Is it because no home's conclusive rest it knows* "

Here the poet conveys his opinion humorously, but more strongly by giving it the form of a question.

The principle of contrast is largely used in the poem for the sake of clearness. *Vide* verses 978-80.

> " *Greatness* humbly bends but *littleness* always
> Spreads out its plumes, and loads itself with praise."

> " *Greatness* is absence of conceit ; *meanness*, we deem
> Riding on car of vanity supreme ".

> " *Greatness* will hide a neighbour's shame ;
> *Meanness* his faults to all the world proclaim".

Reduplication of words occurs for the sake of effect or emphasis : with double meaning,

> " Poyyamai poyyamai yattin aram pira
> Seyyamai seyyamai mantru " 297.

> " Iranthar iranthar anaiyar, sinatthai
> Thuranthar thuranthar thuṇai "—310.

The same words are used with their variants conveying different meanings for alliterative effect.

> " Vahutthan vahuttha vahai yallal, kodi
> Thokuttharkum thuytthal arithu " 377.

" Thupparku thuppaya thuppakki thupparku
Thuppa yathuum maḷai" 12.

Sometimes the upamanam is given without the upameyam ; *vide* 475-6 ' Peeli pei ' and ' Nunik-kombu'. " Too much of peacock feathers will break the bandy axle-tree " " For a climber to venture beyond the tree-top is sure death".

Personifications in brief are largely used :

" Inmai yena oru pavi " *i.e.*, poverty a sinner 142
" Alukkāru ena oru pavi " *i.e.*, envy a sinner.

Personifications are sometimes mixed with rehetorical address ' Malaiyo vallai etc.' 1221.

" Kudi yenum kuntra vilakkam "	401.
" Porul yenum poyya vilakkam "	753.
" Ihal yenum yevva noy "	853.
" Naṉ yenum nallāl "	924.
" Nilam yennum nallāl "	1040.
" Pasi yenum Thee-piṉi "	227.

Telling phrases abound :—

" Sina menum sernthārai kolli, ' *i.e.*, anger a killer of the kindred, 306.

" Kannirku anikalam kannottam "	575.
" Koduthum kolal vendum "	867.
" Nanjunbar Kalluṉpavar "	926.
"Karū maniyil pāvāy "	1123.
" Pan māyak kalvan paṉi moḻi "	1258.
" Kettarku nallar il."	1293.
" Unalinum undathu aral inithu "	1326.
" Ya kāvā rayinum na kakka."	27.

The negative form is preferred for the positive effect :

> " Lute sweet, yal sweet, they will say
> Who haven't heard the baby's prattle "—66

i.e. those who have heard the baby's prattle will not say that the lute is sweet or the yal is sweet.

Sometimes words are placed in juxtaposition with the effect of oxymoron :

> " Vilangodu makkal anaiyar, ilankunul
> Kattrarodu enai yavar ". 410.
>
> " Learning's irradiating grace who gain
> Others excel, as men the bestial train " 410.

Portraits in brief occur which will appear expanded in long stanzas in other poets :

> " Her frame tender shoot, her teeth pearls, her smell fragrance,
> Her eyes darts, her shoulders the bent bamboo " 1113.

Metaphors in brief are scattered all over the poem, 'Kamak-Kanichi' 1251, 'Kamak-Kalan' 605, 'Sol-leruḷavar' 872, etc. The different stages of the love passion in the morning, noon and in the evening are metaphorically represented as bud, flower, and blossom :

> " Kālai *arumbi*, paha lellam *pothūki*
> Mālai *malarum* in noy " 1227.
>
> " My passion at morn a bud, all day an opening flower,
> Full-blown expands in the evening hour " 1227.—

There is no lack of periphrases in Kural. *Vide* chap. 92 for instance on 'Wanton Women'. They are spoken of as 'ay thodiyar' 'porul pendir' 'pothu nalatthar' 'thannalam parippar' 'māya mahalir' and 'iru-mana-pendir'. Thus variety, like brevity, adds zest to poetry. The other beauties and graces of style and diction the reader will appreciate as he goes carefully through the poem.

The careful reader will also note that, while the first two parts of the poem contain ex-cathedral utterances, or authoritative pronouncements, or almost oracular sayings, the third part indulges the gentler graces of art becoming the subject-matter thereof, in the soliloques and dialogues of lovers composing it.

We have said something about the thought and the art of Thiruvalluvar. The poet's mind was pure and his thoughts were high and ennobling and the poet's art was adapted to his thoughts. His inborn aptitude was developed and disciplined by the study of books, and by practice. Thought must be vivified by the imagination, and poetic thought will find for itself smooth and melodious expression. The poet who is an artist possesses that conscious power over language and thought which gives him precision and grace in adapting means to ends and fine discrimination in choosing his resources. Though every work of art must be characterised by precision and perspicuity, by force and beauty of style, there will be found in the highest literary work a grace and freedom that cannot be imparted by rules or attained by mere practice. True genius is nature's dower, and so is true genius for expression to some extent. Our poet had true genius in both forms, and his immortality was therefore assured. His immortal poem has conferred immortality on him, one of the few names that were not born to die; and his immortality grows as often as "they quote" him in every circumstance or situation of life.

APPENDIX.

A Symposium.

"The Kural has strong claim upon our attention, as a part of the literature of the country, and as a work of intrinsic excellence. The author, passing over what is peculiar to particular classes of society and introducing such ideas only as are common to all, has avoided the uninteresting details of observances found in Manu and the other sastras: and thus in general maintains a dignified style. It cannot be supposed necessary for the sake of Christianity to deny to such works whatever degree of merit they may possess. Christianity required not the aid of falsehood or of concealment. Nor need we wish to blacken the system and books of the country beyond what truth will warrant. The Kural itself, esteemed the best book of morals written by a Hindu, is an illustration of this remark".—

Rev. W. H. Drew, 1840.

"The Kural is the masterpiece of Tamil literature—one of the highest and purest expressions of human thought...... ....That which, above all, is wonderful in the Kural is the fact that its author addresses himself, without regard to castes, peoples or beliefs, to the whole community of mankind. The fact that he formulates sovereign morality and absolute reason; that he proclaims in their very essence, in their eternal abstractedness virtue and truth; that he presents, as it were, in one group the highest laws of domestic and social life; that he is equally perfect in thought, in language, and in poetry, in the austere metaphysical contemplation of the great mysteries of the Divine Nature, as in the easy and graceful analysis of the tenderest emotions of the heart".—
M. Ariel to Bucnouf in the Journal Asiatique, Nov.—Dec. 1848.

" Tiruvalluvar is the venerated sage and law-giver of the Tamil people.................There is no trace in the Kural of many things, systems, doctrines and practices, current in South India at different periods, because, I suppose, they had been eliminated from the sage's own eclectic system of faith and practice and because his work is didactic and not controversial. The Kural owes much of its popularity to its exquisite poetic form. Probably the Tamil sage adapted it as being the best representative in Tamil of the Sanskrit sloka. The brevity rendered necessary by the form gives an oracular effect to the utterances of the great Tamil " Master of Sentences ". They are the choicest of moral epigrams............The selection of the most difficult metre in the language—one permitting no deviation from strict rule, and requiring such wonderful condensation—for a long work showed that the author intended to expend upon it his utmost of poetic power and to make it a " Possession for ever, " a " Delight of many generations "..............It is not probable that Tiruvalluvar translated a single sloka from Sanskrit. Kural is certainly *not an anthology*, but the perfect and most elaborate work of one master. The weaver of Mylapore was undoubtedly one of the *great geniuses of the world.* Complete in itself, the sole work of its author, it (the Kural) has come down the stream of ages absolutely uninjured, hardly a single various reading of any importance being found."—*The Rev. Dr. G. U. Pope*, 1886.

The Kural is 'that admirable collection of stanzas in the Tamil language, which is instinct with the purest and most elevated religious emotion.........What philosophy he teaches seems to be of the eclectic school as represented by the Baghavadgita. '—*Dr. Barth, Religions of India*, 1882.

" There are two books in India which have taken entire possession of the hearts and minds of the people: the first of these is the *Ramayana* of Tulasidas, which is known to every peer and peasant in Northern India, and the other is the *Kural* of Thiruvalluvar which is equally well-known throughout the south of the Indian peninsula. The authors of both these works were essentially moralists and monotheists, and their poems have moulded the characters and guided the lives of many generations of their countrymen. It is the pride of both poets that their works are absolutely pure, and it is creditable to the Hindu community that the two works, which are free from even an indelicate allusion, have become the most popular books of India, and for hundreds of years have held undisputed sway over the people. Of the two, the Kural is much the older."—*Frederick Pincott*, 1908.

" As regards the Kural itself, it stands on its merits. The purity of its Tamil, the richness of its diction, the lofty tone of its morality, the theistic and unsectarian nature of its theology, the endless variety of topics discussed in its one hundred and thirty-three chapters, and the profound esteem in which it is held by all classes of Tamil-speaking Hindus are too well-known to need praise or comment". —*W. P. Coomarasamy.*

"The Kural is a Tamil poem on ethical subjects, held in the highest estimation by the Tamil people............The text itself is simple and readily yields its meaning to the diligent student. But as there is a " pleasure in poetic pains which only poets know," so in this matchless piece of poetic effort there are depths of thought and heights of moral excellence which can only be perceived by those endowed with a sense for the true and the beautiful in life. Though universally known and frequently quoted, the Kural is not studied as intensely as it ought to be by the Tamil people."—*The Rev. Dr. Lazarus*, 1892.

"At its very birth it (the Kural) received the highest encomiums of the proudest scholars of the day, the Pandits of the far-famed Madura College or Sangam............One of the Collegians compares it to the Veda, and another says that, unlike the Veda, Thiruvalluvar's words do not lose their merit by anybody repeating them. One speaks of it as containing everything worth knowing, and another that there is nothing which is not contained in this work. One says that the words are sweeter than the heavenly Ambrosia, and that, unlike the latter, they can be partaken of by everybody. And as the poet utters these words, even our own mouth begins to water. Another says that they are sweet food to the mind, sweet to the ear, and sweet to the tongue and the great panacea for the ills of karma. One compares it to the sun which, dispelling the deep darkness of ignorance, makes the lotus of the heart bloom forth. Another compares it to the lamps dispelling our mental darkness of ignorance with the oil-can of dharma, the wick of artha, and the ghee of kama, words of affection as the flame, and the short metre as the lamp stand. Its brevity not bordering on unintelligibility or ambiguity as do most of the Sutras in Sanskrit, its perfection of expression and style and its deepness are all matters taken up for praise by those learned collegians. And what is more, the poet Kalladar brings out in his verse its most prominent character, its universality. People wrangle about this or that being the truth, and they range themselves into various schools, but all are agreed about the truth of the verse uttered by Thiruvalluvar. And, since his time, all religionists, Buddhists and Jains, Saivas and Vaishnávas, have all claimed him as their own; we need not enquire wherefrom he derived his truths. It is enough to acknowledge that it is perfection of truth, if one can say so, a perfect ethical and religious Code, a perfection of art and thought.—*J. M. Nallaswami Pillai*, 1921.

Printed by Solden & Co., Madras, S.E.